SUPERBIKES

MACHINES OF DREAMS

Phil West

igloo

igloo

Published in 2006
by Igloo Books Ltd
Cottage Farm,
Sywell,
NN6 0JB.
www.igloo-books.com

ISBN 1-84561-422-4

Project managed by: Metro Media Ltd
Editorial and design management: Cecilia Thom
Author: Phil West
Sub-Editor: Adam Phillips
Layout: Z Swaleh, Cecilia Thom
Cover: Tom Lynton, Joel Rojas
Pictures contributed by: Aprilia, Benelli, Bimota, BMW, Buell,
Confederate, MV Agusta, Ducati, Harley-Davidson, Honda, Kawasaki,
Norton, Suzuki, Titan, Triumph, Victory, Yamaha, Alastair Walker
Printed in China

Contents

The ultimate has always had a special appeal, whether that be the biggest, the most powerful or simply the fastest. In the automotive world there are cars... and then there are supercars. It is the supercars whose performances excite the most, whose mouth-watering styling bewitches the eye and whose lavish luxury and exclusivity has the most cachet. Those are the cars most of us want and lust after, even if we will never be able to afford them.

The same is true when it comes to motorcycling. Bikers have long been a breed apart: individuals with a rebel spirit who are happy to embrace danger and discomfort for the unique thrills biking brings. Superbikes, with their single-minded pursuit of performance and often dazzling, razor-edged styling, are the ultimate manifestation of that.

Some people want a superbike as a kind of trophy; the pleasure comes from simple ownership. But to most, the superbike is *the best*. And for those who crave motorcycling in its purest, most thrill-laden form, only the best will do. What's more, unlike supercars, many superbikes are within our financial reach. The biggest and best jewels in the automotive world often start on the wrong side of six figures, but many of the planet's leading superbikes can be had for under five.

We've Honda, in the main, to thank for that. The Japanese giant's astonishing CB750 of 1968 not only became known as the first 'superbike' – thanks to its combination of unique large capacity four-cylinder engine, 125mph+ performance, lavish levels of equipment and high build quality – but was also respectably affordable too. So successful was it that all the Far Eastern rivals that followed Honda's lead stayed true to the same recipe, and do so even today.

That's not the whole story, however. The Europeans, with their myriad snaking roads, at first fought back with machines that emphasized handling prowess rather than brute power. The Americans, with their arrow-straight highways and hot-rod culture, favored big, lazy engines and laid-back style. As a result, nearly 30 years on, there's never been a larger, more varied or more potent and exciting array of superbikes on offer. There are those whose performance can blow your mind, whose sheer beauty bedazzles and whose engineering brilliance can rank with the best from the racing world. A few even offer all three at the same time.

This book is a tribute to, and celebration of, these machines. From superbikes that are within the budget of many, to virtual one-offs that can't be bought for love nor money, the motorcycling masterpieces featured here show that the state of the superbike is more exciting and desirable than ever. Just one question remains – if these bikes are the pinnacle of modern motorcycling, just what have we got to look forward to in the future?

The History of the Superbike

With vibrant, exciting, enthralling machines now being produced in Japan, USA, Europe and beyond, there has never been a better time for superbike fans to indulge their passion for motorcycling excellence. But it has taken nearly three decades of evolution and development by the planet's greatest bike designers and engineers to get to this point. Here we present a selection of the highlights of the superbike's emergence, since its creation in the late 1960s...

Honda
CB750

The first large capacity, multi-cylinder production machine from the Far East changed the whole direction and power base of modern motorcycling. Although four-cylinder engines are common today (as are its disc brakes; electric, instead of kick, starters; and 125mph-plus performance), in 1968 these things had never before been seen on one machine.

The Honda CB750 changed all that. It set new standards of performance and reliability in the large capacity class, as well as raising the bar for equipment levels, quality and versatility. In short, it was the first superbike.

Its story is a fascinating one: in 1966, after celebrating its fifth successive GP world championship, Honda took the radical decision

to pull out of sportbikes and, instead, turned its attention to the development of high-performance consumer machines utilizing the technology it had developed through racing.

Honda's biggest bike at that point was the Dream CB450, a high-performance DOHC twin created at the request of Honda America. Now, it seemed, the USA wanted more. At that time the 650cc displacement was the largest to be found in Japan. Honda also learned that Britain's Triumph was developing a high-performance model with a three-cylinder 750cc engine, while Harley Davidson's maximum output machine produced 66bhp. These three factors formed the outline of Honda's new larger cc model: it would be driven by a 750cc four-cylinder engine with a maximum output of 67bhp.

When publicly unveiled at the Tokyo Motor Show in October 1966, the CB750 Four was a huge hit and rave reviews began pouring in. The production version was released in the USA in January 1969 at a retail price of $1,495. Competing European and American large bikes of the time were selling for between $2,800 and $4,000.

Naturally, the CB was a huge success. In fact, such was demand for the machine that Honda had to quickly revise its production schedules. Initially the target was to produce 1,500 a month; that changed to being a monthly figure and soon even that was insufficient. It finally doubled to 3,000.

But the CB was not just a commercial success, it was victorious on the track too. In August 1969 Honda's racing team entered four CB750s in the Suzuka 10-hour endurance race and came away with a one–two finish. Meanwhile, in the USA, veteran rider Dick Mann snatched victory at the Daytona 200 in March 1970 on one of the first racing CBs, a result that sent customers throughout the USA running to Honda dealers.

In short, the CB was a monumental success – so much so that it cemented Honda's path to world domination and forced all rivals to follow its lead.

Specifications	
Engine	736cc
Max power	67bhp
Max torque	45lb/ft
St 1/4 mile	12.7 seconds
Top speed	124mph

Kawasaki Z1 (1972)

Honda's CB750 may have been the first superbike, but Kawasaki were not that far behind. In fact, as Big H unveiled its multi-cylinder wonder, Kawasaki was already well advanced with a 750-4 of its own. Beaten to the drop, Kawasaki modified its plans, producing – instead of a single overhead cam 750-4 – a double overhead cam 900. The legendary Z1 of 1972 was the result.

With more power than the CB, the Z1 was the superbike king on both the road and the track for years to come, posting numerous speed records and track victories.

The big Kawasaki may have had questionable handling and minimal brakes, but its powerhouse engine was superbike 'top dog' and remained the basis of numerous variants up to 1,100cc for over 10 years.

Specifications	
Engine	903cc
Max power	82bhp
Max torque	52lb/ft
St 1/4 mile	12.2 seconds
Top speed	131mph

Ducati 750 Super Sport (1974)

driven camshafts, as developed by the legendary designer Fabio Taglioni, for 15 years when it decided to move into the big bike market. The first product, effectively a 750 comprising two singles mounted in a longitudinal 90-degree formation, was the GT750 in 1971. But the definitive event that changed the destiny of the marque came a year later when a racer, derived from this production machine and ridden by Briton, Paul Smart, beat the world's best at the prestigious Imola 200.

In production, the GT was followed by the unfaired 750 Sport in 1973 which, in turn, was followed by this, the 750 Super Sport (or SS). This was, in spirit and style, a true replica of the Paul Smart machine. The SS certainly succeeded in its prime objective of delivering superlative all-round performance – so much so that it even became a favorite with racers – but it also offered much more than that. Its charismatic and unique Desmodromic V-twin was both characterful and potent, and the bike was truly versatile and desireable. Ducatis would never be the same again.

Specifications

Engine	748cc
Max power	72bhp
Max torque	52.8lb/ft
St 1/4 mile	12.9 seconds
Top speed	120mph

Today Ducati are renowned the world over as the definitive Italian manufacturer of V-twin sports machines, with a racing pedigree, particularly in the World Superbike Championship. But it is the first of these, the 750 Super Sport of 1974, that set the standard for all to follow and truly put Ducati on the map.

The Bologna firm had been building single-cylinder machines with revolutionary Desmodromic shaft-

Honda CBX1000
(1978)

If the four-cylinder SOHC Honda CB750 had wowed the world in 1968, its spiritual yet audacious successor was the six-cylinder double overhead camshaft CBX1000 of 1978. Even at standstill it was magnificent: its huge and handsome six-cylinder powerplant resembled a metal sculpture more than a motorcycle. And on the move it was quite unlike anything else, delivering unique, smooth power – and lots of it.

By any measure it was an astonishing feat of engineering. Despite its phenomenal performance and manners, however, it was a commercial failure, deemed too big, too heavy and too expensive in a world now dominated by refined and potent fours.

Nearly 20 years on, however, the monster CBX lives on as one of the most desirable and collectable of all Honda superbikes. Few machines since have matched its engineering ambition and iconic status.

Specifications	
Engine	1,047cc
Max power	105bhp
Max torque	52.27lb/ft
St 1/4 mile	12.2 seconds
Top speed	135mph

Kawasaki Z1300

Only Kawasaki would dare rival Honda's awesome CBX1000-6 but, with the spectacular Z1300 of 1979, it did just that. And more.

The word 'more' sums up the whole Z13 ethos. Although matching the CBX's transverse six-cylinder with double overhead camshafts layout, everything else about the big Kawasaki was an exercise in unique excess. First it had watercooling (radical in itself in 1979) to allow closer engineering tolerances and higher performance. It was also a full 1,286cc (222ccs more than the CBX) and benefited from fuel injection – the sum total of which was enough to generate a massive 120bhp and 135mph. The Z13 was massive physically, too, weighing in at 653lbs. This made it cumbersome and far too much of a handful for most. Classic though the Z1300 may be, it's also a perfect example that bigger is not always best.

Specifications

Engine	1,286cc
Max power	120bhp
Max torque	86lb/ft
St 1/4 mile	12.1s seconds
Top speed	135mph

Honda
CX500 Turbo

Honda started the brief fashion for turbocharging when it introduced the CX500 Turbo in 1981. Based on the humble but technically advanced and versatile CX500, it boasted a textbook full of technological advances. Not least among these was Honda's first fuel-injection system – the PGM-FI injection system, which only became commonplace on Honda motorcycles from the late 1990s, is derived from it – but there was also anti-dive front forks, a monoshock rear suspension system and an extremely efficient and stylish (for the times) touring fairing with novel faired-in indicators.

So not only was the CX500 Turbo a massive accomplishment, it had been a huge undertaking by Big H. But the most compelling measure of its success was the simple fact that the CX500 Turbo worked well, too. Here was a 497cc machine capable nearly 130mph – unheard of in 1981. What's more it was comfortable, sophisticated and even handled reasonably for a 518lb machine. Of course, the CX500 Turbo was never going to be a commercial success. At a price virtually double that of conventional superbikes and all based on a bike – the CX – that to sports bike fans had all the

appeal of a scooter, it was impossible. But it did cause such a wave of excitement and technical interest that it inspired a whole wave of turbos from rival manufacturers.

Today, the CX Turbo may yet to achieve quite the classic status it deserves. But with a sheaf of technical advances to rival Honda's own NR750, performance that was simply beyond belief, and for causing such a wave of all things turbo in the early 1980s, that day can surely not be far off.

Specifications	
Engine	497cc
Max power	82bhp
Max torque	58lb/ft
St 1/4 mile	12.3 seconds
Top speed	128mph

Kawasaki GPz900R Ninja

Eleven years after the introduction of the Z1, Kawasaki revolutionized the bike world again. In 1983 the all-new GPz900R Ninja tore up the superbike rulebook, re-defined the capabilities of a liter-bike and wowed the world.

Kawasaki unveiled the new GPz900R at the 1983 Paris Show, and then invited the world's press to Laguna Seca raceway in December to ride it. Its performance blew everyone away. Not only did the GPz claim the title 'World's Fastest' by recording over 150mph and a standing quarter mile in just under 11 seconds, it handled like no other superbike before. It didn't take long before the GPz became the best-selling bike in the world, not to mention claiming numerous 'Bike of the Year' titles in many countries.

The simple explanation for its success was the beginning of the quest to marry traditional superbike power with the handling of smaller, lighter machines. The GPz was designed from the outset to not only be monumentally powerful, but to cradle that power in a slim, light, strong and compact rolling chassis. That's why its all-new engine was watercooled with a cam drive on the right-hand side of the cylinder for extreme narrowness. And why it also boasted state-of-the-art suspension (monoshock rear, anti-dive forks front), brakes and aerodynamics. They got it so right that, not only was the GPz the basis for all Kawasaki superbikes up to the mid-1990s, it also became the inspiration and basic template for virtually all superbikes since.

Specifications	
Engine	908cc
Max power	115bhp
Max torque	63lb/ft
St 1/4 mile	10.90 seconds
Top speed	150mph

Suzuki
GSX-R750

Other manufacturers may have flirted with ultra-light weight allied to immense power, but it was Suzuki, with its iconic first GSX-R750 in 1985, that changed forever the basic superbike mantra.

Its inspiration was the 1982 Endurance World Championship-winning GS1000R XR41 works racer. Its key feature was to have a revolutionary ultra-lightweight aluminum frame. In itself, aluminum frames were nothing new; the appeal was that, in theory, an aluminum frame was lighter and stronger than the steel-tube units that were then the status quo. The problem was producing an aluminum frame that could handle relatively high horsepower in a cost-effective manner.

With the GSX-R, Suzuki engineers learned to incorporate aluminum castings along with extruded tubes to reduce the number of parts needed for a frame. A typical steel frame of the time had around 90 parts, the radically new GSX-R just 26.

When the GSX-R750 was unveiled at the 1984 IFMA motorcycle show in Cologne it looked like no superbike ever built. Instead, it bore such a close resemblance to the XR41 endurance racer it was, to all intents and purposes, the world's first production 'racer replica'.

The GSX-R's aluminum frame followed the lines of the racer's steel-tube item very closely, as did its dual headlights. And that racing heritage was also why the GSX-R sported an 18-inch front wheel at a time when 16-inch items were in fashion. That exotic aluminum frame, meanwhile, weighed a mere 18lbs, 19 fewer than the 1975 GS750's steel-tube arrangement, and cost just $100 more to produce.

Another reason for the light weight was the use of oil cooling. Air-cooled engines' performance were limited by heat, but Suzuki engineers felt water-cooling added too much weight and complication. So why not use the oil already in the sump? Suzuki identified the most critical areas to be cooled, increased the oil capacity, developed a dual-stage oil pump, and called it the Suzuki Advanced Cooling System (SACS).

This cooling system also helped boost the power by allowing smaller, lighter pistons and higher compression. Flat slide carburetors, as used until then in motocrossers, were used to improve throttle response and fuel atomization. Finally, the new GSX-R also featured the Twin Swirl Combustion Chamber (TSCC) head design introduced on the 1980 GS1100.

All of this added up to a radical, race-ready looking machine with a dry weight of just 388lbs (2lbs under the then AMA Superbike minimum weight limit) and boasting a claimed 106bhp. Both numbers were revolutionary in terms of power-to-weight and although that power figure was still 5bhp behind that of Yamaha's new five-valve FZ750, the GSX-R weighed 55lbs less than the FZ and nearly 100lbs less than Honda's VF750F Interceptor.

In terms of straight-line speed, the Suzuki made up for having less power by having less mass, and equalled the Yamaha in the quarter-mile and top speed. In terms of cornering, its two closest rivals came nowhere near. The new Suzuki was the superbike to have on the road and the track.

Specifications

Engine	748cc
Max power	100bhp
Max torque	54lb/ft
St 1/4 mile	11.2 seconds
Top speed	147mph

Yamaha FZR1000R EXUP

After many years chasing the pack, Yamaha returned to the top of the superbike pile with its FZR1000 Genesis, which debuted its Deltabox frame system, in 1987. But it was its successor in 1989, the FZR1000R EXUP, which became the superbike king of the early 1990s.

The EXUP boasted the whole box of four-stroke tricks Yamaha had developed over the previous decade. It had the Genesis' revolutionary extruded aluminum twin-spar 'Deltabox' frame. Its water-cooled engine had the slant block, 20-valve layout pioneered by the FZ750, yet, at 1,002cc, it was even more potent than the 125bhp 989cc Genesis. Best of all, it had an electronically-operated exhaust valve, the EXUP system, which became the shorthand for referring to the king Yamaha for years to come.

The use of this system resulted not only in a healthy boost to mid-range performance, but also increased peak output to 140bhp. At the same time, the bike's chassis was completely revamped, significantly improving the handling so that it became the best of Japan's superbikes. At least until the arrival of Honda's FireBlade…

Specifications

Engine	1,002cc
Max power	140bhp
Max torque	78.9lb/ft
St 1/4 mile	10.1 seconds
Top speed	171mph

Kawasaki ZZ-R1100

By 1990, Kawasaki had already built a long line of classic powerful in-line four-cylinder four stroke fours, with a pedigree steeped in bikes like the Z1 and GPz900R. So when the new ZZ-R1100 came out it had a lot to live up to.

The ZZ-R was neither a no-holds-barred sportster nor an outright tourer, but it still gained a huge following among admirers of its hugely powerful yet silky-smooth engine. In original, restricted form (due to a 'gentleman's agreement between the Japanese factories) the big, GPz900R-derived powerplant was good for 125bhp. Later, unrestricted versions boasted 147bhp – enough for the big Kawasaki to power from 20mph in top gear up to a world-leading 175mph in one strong surge.

Everything about the ZZ-R was massive, from its wide 180-section rear tyre to the huge 320mm front brake discs. But despite all that power and weight, riders found the ZZ-R easy to handle, thanks mostly to its huge aluminum perimeter frame and excellent suspension. The ZZ-R was not only the world's fastest production bike; it was an excellent all-rounder, a peerless package that remained on top for six years.

Specifications	
EnEngine	1,052cc
Max power	147bhp
Max torque	81.1lb/ft
St 1/4 mile	10.1 seconds
Top speed	175mph

Norton F1

By the late 1980s this legendary British marque was a pale shadow of the glorious giant that dominated world racing in the 1940s and 1950s. After the industrial collapse in the 1970s and a series of buyouts, all that remained was a small factory and a number of projects centered on novel rotary wankel engines.

On the track, however, all was not lost. The pinnacle achievements of these times was the domination of the British Superbike Championship in 1989–1991 in JPS-sponsored, black-liveried machines, together with a glorious victory in the 1991 Senior TT in the hands of Steve Hislop.

On the road, the most glorious product was the limited edition Norton F1 superbike, powered by a road version of the controversial 588cc wankel and dressed in racer-replicating black and gold bodywork.

On the surface it had it all: a superb bespoke aluminum twin-spar frame, top-notch WP suspension at the front and rear, equally impressive Brembo brakes, slinky styling by British designers Seymour-Powell, and the dimensions and performance to threaten all comers. In reality it was under-developed and unreliable, its performance, though able, was unstartling and it all cost a then-massive £13,000. Fabulous ornament, though.

Specifications

Engine	588cc
Max power	95bhp
Max torque	57lb/ft
St 1/4 mile	12.5 seconds
Top speed	135mph

Honda CBR900RR FireBlade

The launch of Honda's original FireBlade, the CBR900RR, in 1992, simply revolutionized the superbike world. And what made it an even bigger shock was that no-one had seen it coming. Until then, Big H had largely been perceived as a producer of more leisurely, luxurious and touring-orientated machinery. Its only liter-class sportsbike of the time, after all, was the heavy and cumbersome CBR1000F sports-tourer.

Until then, if riders wanted a fierce Japanese superbike, they turned to Yamaha's FZR1000R EXUP or Suzuki's GSX-R1100. The key to the FireBlade's potency was its astonishingly light weight. Its an oft-repeated cliché today, but the Blade delivered liter-class power in a 600cc-sized package. There was no revolutionary technology

in delivering that: the 893cc transverse four was impressively compact, but that in itself was nothing radical – nor was the beefy twin-spar aluminum frame. What did change the whole culture of superbike development, however, was its fastidiuous attention to detail and relentless mass-saving. Even the upper fairing cowl had holes drilled in it to save precious grams.

The Blade's impact on the superbike class in 1992 was total: Honda went from not even being recognized as a superbike producer, to being the manufacturer of *the* machine to own.

The FireBlade's amazing power-to-weight ratio wasn't bettered until Yamaha's equally radical, but derivative, R1 of 1998...

Specifications	
Engine	893cc
Max power	122bhp
Max torque	65lb/ft
St 1/4 mile	10.3 seconds
Top speed	165mph

Yamaha YZF1000 R1 (1998)

Yamaha's astonishing first R1 of 1997 may have finally dethroned the amazing FireBlade, but it did it by stealing a leaf out of Honda's book. If the key to the Blade was power allied to light weight, Yamaha did exactly the same, only more so.

When unveiled to the world's press in an amazingly theatrical presentation involving world superbike star Scott Russell, the introduction saw just two numbers flashed on a big screen: 150bhp and 175kg. They said it all. What amazed even further was how well those claims gelled and worked together.

The R1 did everything right and nothing wrong. It had a brawny motor, a solid and well-balanced chassis, dialed-in suspension and fantastic brakes. The Yamaha YZF-R1 changed the rules by successfully combining the awesome power available previously in open-class size with the light weight and responsiveness that a 600-class chassis affords. Admittedly Honda had been there first with the Blade, but that was, by no means, mechanically nor stylistically, the quantum leap forward of the R1.

Specifications

Engine	998cc
Max power	150bhp
Max torque	79.9lb/ft
St 1/4 mile	10.3 seconds
Top speed	173.25mph

Suzuki
GSX-R1000 K1

Up to the turn of the millennium, Suzuki's GSX-R750 was its best effort at rivalling Honda's FireBlade and Yamaha's R1. Although the Gixxer, as it became known, had brilliant handling, however, there was no getting away from the fact that it gave away 250cc to its rival. That all changed in 2000.

With its new GSX-R1000, Suzuki came mightily close to the holy grail of a 1bhp/kg power-to-weight ratio. Chiming in at a paltry 4kg more than the 750, but producing in excess of 160bhp at the crank, it equated to 0.94bhp/kg, a figure that comfortably beat the R1's 0.84bhp/kg. That, allied to a typical GSX-R sublime chassis, added up to what many instantly regarded as the best superbike in the world.

Outwardly, the big GSX-R was identical to the 750. It shared the same wheelbase of 1,410mm and its rake and trail figures were identical too (at 24° and 96mm respectively), giving the 1000 everything required for sharp yet predictable handling. In early 2000 there wasn't just a new century to deal with, there was a new superbike king.

Specifications

Engine	988cc
Max power	160bhp
Max torque	81lb/ft
St 1/4 mile	10.1 seconds
Top speed	180mph

The Modern Superbike

On the following pages is the very latest and best in world superbikes, the culmination of nearly 40 years of evolution, design genius and inspired engineering. From racetrack refugees to the wildest of street cruisers, every one of the bikes included here offers true bike fans a treasure trove of engineering delicacies with which to gorge themselves upon: styling that stops you dead in your tracks, performance that simply blows away anything else on the road, and riding thrills that are without equal. Step into the world of the ultimate superbikes.

The original FireBlade of 1992 changed superbikes forever. This latest version is back on top with an incomparable yet mouth-watering mix of potency and aplomb

There are few names in motorcycling as well recognized, long lived and revered as the single word 'Fireblade'. Fourteen years (including more than a few in the doldrums) after the original Blade astonished the motorcycling world with its convention-defying package of 1,000cc performance in an ultra-lightweight and compact package, Honda's very latest 2006 version is back where it belongs: right at the very top of the superbike class.

Honda CBR1000RR Fireblade

It's worth noting straight away that these two bikes – the first and latest Blades – share just two things: the name and the peerless way they despatch any rival. Such is the speed of progress in this most competitive and technologically advanced motorcycle category that everything has moved on in leaps and bounds. Tyres are fatter and stickier; suspension, braking and frame technology is a quantum leap beyond what went before; and performance figures speak for themselves. The first Blade produced around 110bhp at the rear wheel, enough to propel it to some 150mph. Its latest descendent has nearer 160 and 180 respectively, to say nothing of the awesome ease with which it despatches corners.

The new 2006 CBR1000RR is Honda's most complete road-going sports-bike package since producing the original Blade way back in 1992. And Honda has achieved all this by weaving together fun, reliability, racetrack ability and style.

But what truly sets this latest Blade apart is its sheer, polished refinement and ease of use. It may sound absurd but this road-going motorcycle – whose performance is closer to that of an F1 car than a conventional motorcycle – is civilized and so easy to ride it's almost novice friendly. Where its closest rivals (the Kawasaki ZX-10R, Suzuki GSX-R1000K6 and Yamaha R1) all, to varying degrees, sometimes demand an expert rider's hand, the Honda confounds by delivering a Jekyll-and-Hyde mix of calm ease along with rabid (yet completely controllable), explosive performance.

The new CBR is ridiculously easy to just jump on and ride fast. The character and 'edge' for which previous variants were criticized has been replaced with accomplished buckets of fun. It wheelies everywhere if the mood should take you (requiring only the merest dip of the clutch and twist of the right wrist in the first four gears), is stable mid-corner, turns easily, is simplicity itself to ride around town and has excellent brakes. What's more, it's characterized by excellent build quality, superb components and a classy, understated style that ensures it will hold its price.

The CBR1000RR is the bike that satisfies every type of riding skill (fast or medium pace on the road, hard-core or novice on the track) and is now made all the better for having added attitude. Welcome back Blade, you've been missed.

What's in a name?

To be strictly accurate, the latest Blade doesn't share the name of the original CBR of 1992. That bike was called the FireBlade, the latest is simply the Fireblade, with no upper case 'B' in the middle.

HESD

It stands for Honda Electronic Steering Damper – a first on any superbike, replacing the hydraulic items was commonplace until now. It works by being constantly variable with damping force rising and lowering according to road speed. Clever or what?

It's in the family

If you're unfamiliar with road machines but think you've seen those lines somewhere before, you're probably right: the Blade's styling mimics that of Honda's phenomenal V5-powered RC211V MotoGP machine. As does, incidentally, the Blade's road-going little brother, the CBR600RR.

Size matters

Not all Fireblades have been 1,000cc. The first, 14 years ago, was nominally 900 but was actually 893cc. Over successive models this grew first to 918cc, then to 954 and, finally, to today's 998. The quest for performance allows for no waste.

Father of the Blade

The creative genius credited with the Blade concept (essentially the minimal weight, by producing a 1,000cc superbike with the weight of a 600 and dimensions of a 400) was Tadao Baba who, until his recent retirement, was significantly involved in all subsequent Fireblade development.

Specifications

Engine	Fuel-injected 16-valve transverse four
Chassis	Aluminum beam frame
Displacement	998cc
Maximum power	153.1bhp
Maximum torque	76.3lb/ft
Transmission	Six gears
Standing 1/4 mile	10.66 seconds
Terminal speed	140.05mph
Maximum speed	173.3mph
Brakes, front	2 x 320mm discs, four-piston calipers
Brakes, rear	220mm disc, single-piston caliper
Suspension, front	43mm inverted forks, fully adjustable
Suspension, rear	Monoshock, fully adjustable
Dry weight	176kg/388lb
Wheelbase	1,400mm/55in
Fuel capacity	18ltr/4.76 US gall
Seat height	831mm/32.7in
Tyres, front	120/70 x 17
Tyres, rear	190/50 x 17
Price	£8,899/US$11,299

...the Honda confounds by delivering a Jekyll-and-Hyde mix of calm ease along with rabid, explosive performance

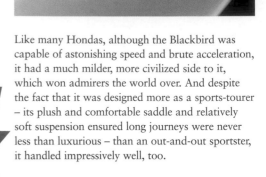

It took six years for a machine to rival the original speed king Kawasaki ZZ-R1100. But when it arrived, what a machine it was...

Motorcycle manufacturers have always yearned to produce the fastest bike on the planet. In the early 1990s Kawasaki claimed the crown with its ZZ-R1100 and it wasn't until 1996 that Honda was able to counter with its awesome Super Blackbird.

The name is derived from the stealth American warplane and is entirely appropriate. When first unveiled, the world was in awe of the awesomely

Honda CBR1100XX Super Blackbird

fast and moody CBR1100XX. The 1,137cc engine was good for a claimed 164bhp, and that, plus the fact that it was held in a super-aerodynamic chassis weighing 241kg (531lb), resulted in a machine with a top speed of nearly 170mph. In short, the Super Blackbird was at the time, not only the most powerful production motorcycle on the market, but also the fastest.

Like many Hondas, although the Blackbird was capable of astonishing speed and brute acceleration, it had a much milder, more civilized side to it, which won admirers the world over. And despite the fact that it was designed more as a sports-tourer – its plush and comfortable saddle and relatively soft suspension ensured long journeys were never less than luxurious – than an out-and-out sportster, it handled impressively well, too.

Three years on, in 1999, Honda's flagship was updated and got even better. Initially only a few modifications were obvious, but they were there. The most significant of these was the new fuel-injection system, in place of the previous model's conventional carburetors, coupled to a ram air system. These changes only made a minor difference to peak performance (peak bhp, for example, only rose by 2bhp to 164bhp), but they significantly changed the power delivery, smoothing it across the rev range and eradicating the slight flat spot that had blighted the original. Other changes included subtly revised bodywork (to incorporate the ram air intakes) and a useful larger fuel tank.

Unfortunately, good things don't last forever and what Honda hadn't reckoned on was the introduction in the same year (1999) of Suzuki's all-new rival for the speed crown, the GSX1300R Hayabusa. That said, seven years further down the line, the Blackbird lives on and retains a strong, faithful following.

The Blackbird may no longer be speed top dog but it still offers a virtually unique blend of hyper-performance allied with comfort and practicality. Life on the big Honda is relaxed and roomy; it's great for pillions too thanks to the smooth power delivery, excellent wind protection and wide seat. It may now lack the ultimate rush of newer rivals such as the Hayabusa and Kawasaki's new ZZR1400, but the big Bird is flexible, reliable, practical, proven – and yet can still virtually melt your mind the moment you open the throttle.

Fly me, I'm Honda

The Super Blackbird name is no coincidence. It was a direct 'homage' to the super fast USAF stealth bomber and Honda decided to mimic the aircraft even further by releasing the first Blackbirds in a satin black colorscheme.

It's the FireBlade's big brother...

Although many assume the Super Blackbird's stupendous 164bhp powerplant to be an all-new, purpose-built design, it was actually derived from that of its little sports-bike brother, the then CBR900RR FireBlade. Enlarged, swept volume increased capacity to 1,137cc and it was also fitted with two balancer shafts to reduce vibration.

Nose job

When originally launched in 1996 the Blackbird's frontal aspect was unlike any other motorcycle on the road. The quest for ultimate top speed had forced Honda to adopt a, for the time, fairly radical but aerodynamic shape for the CBR, which demanded as narrow a frontal area as possible. That in turn dictated the novel and unusual-looking stacked headlights arrangement.

Faired-in indicators

The quest for speed led Honda to take some extreme measures, not least with the Super Blackbird's aerodynamics. No detail was overlooked – which is why the indicators were faired into the front mirrors and the front mudguard is deeply valanced.

Safety first

The CBR1100RRXX was also one of the first bikes to be equipped with Honda's electronic immobilizer system, or HISS. This works by incorporating a little electronic device in the key; if the wrong key is used, the bike won't start.

Specifications

Engine	Fuel-injected 16-valve transverse four
Chassis	Aluminum twin-spar frame
Displacement	1,137cc
Maximum power	136.07bhp
Maximum torque	79.86ft/lb
Transmission	Six-speed
Standing 1/4 mile	10.63 seconds
Terminal speed	142.03mph
Maximum speed	167mph
Brakes, front	2 x 310mm discs, three-piston calipers
Brakes, rear	256mm disc, three-piston caliper
Suspension, front	43m forks, adjustable for pre-load
Suspension, rear	Single shock, adjustable for rebound damping and pre-load
Dry weight	224kg/494lb
Wheelbase	1,490mm/58.6in
Fuel capacity	18ltr/4.76 US gall
Seat height	810mm/31.9in
Tyres, front	120/70 x 17
Tyres, rear	180/55 x 17
Price	£8,649 (not on sale in USA)

Ninja

The long-awaited first ZX-10R of 2004 was bold, beautiful and blisteringly quick. The latest version is better yet...

For the best part of a decade Kawasaki had resisted the temptation to re-enter the superbike class. Through the first half of the 1990s its ZZ-R1100 was the undisputed speed king. Yet in persevering with its rapidly aging ZXR750 (later ZX-7R) as its sole big sportster, Big K simply hadn't a 1,000cc sportsbike with which to rival the Honda FireBlade and, later, the Yamaha R1, which went on to dominate the class.

Kawasaki ZX-10R

That all changed with the long-awaited arrival of just such a machine in 2004. The pretty ZX-10R wasn't just capable and powerful, it had a wild reputation too. With razor-sharp steering, big power and very little weight, the big Kawasaki was easily the best of all the road-going superbikes around a racetrack. But on the road it was a machine that demanded nerves of steel, shaking its head over bumps at three-figure speeds – not the best way to keep your heart rate down.

But better still was yet to come. An all-new, restyled and revamped ZX-10R was the most eagerly anticipated 1,000cc sportsbike of 2006, particularly following Kawasaki's claims that its new bike was not only more civilized (thanks in part to having an Ohlins steering damper fitted as standard), it was even quicker, too. Those claims were borne out in the first magazine reviews.

Dyno testing revealed the ZX-10R's power was up from 147bhp at the rear wheel of the old model to a class-leading and GSX-R1000-slaying 161.7bhp. What's more, on race circuits it retained its mantle of the track king where it was still the bike to beat and faster than all of its superbike rivals.

The new ZX-10R is 5kg heavier than the old model, and on the track this extra bulk is always apparent. But despite not being quite as light and nimble as its predecessor, its sheer horsepower lets it demolish the longest of straights in nanoseconds. What's more, that extra steadiness means that the new ZX-10R's handling is solid and secure, too, and there's lots of feeling for how the rear tyre is coping when you get on the throttle, a good thing with a bike with this much power.

On the road the new ZX-10R is also far more stable than before – almost too stable... so much so that some consider that the Kawasaki had lost its wild charismatic edge. And then there are the new looks, which many consider lack the beauty of the original, particularly from the rear with its odd, upswept twin silencers. But these are minor criticisms. The new ZX-10R is arguably the fastest, most potent superbike ever built – certainly on the track. And on the road there are few means of despatching distance as surgically fast and with excitement rather than drama.

Beauty and the beast

The ZX-10R is the most visually striking machine in its class, thanks to a unique combination of dainty, understated nose (because of the novel use of four projector headlights) and, at the rear, a distinctive arrangement of twin upswept silencers.

Power

The big Kawasaki's fuel-injected transverse four is, arguably, the most potent and exhilarating of all 1,000cc sportsbikes. Cam timing and engine management changes have resulted in a top-end rush like no other, although there's now little power down low so you have to rev it more when you want to get a move on. By comparison, the Suzuki GSX-R1000 and Honda FireBlade feel like grunty V-twins...

What's in a name?

It's not just the ZX-10R, it's the ZX-10R Ninja, a name Kawasaki has reserved for it's most exhilarating sportsbikes since the machine that started it all, the GPz900R Ninja of 1984. Respect is due.

Wheelbarrow handles?

Kawasaki replaced the 4:1 exhaust system of the old ZX-10R with a pair of controversial, upswept dual silencers at a time when the class norm preferred underseat cans or MotoGP-style side-exiting pipes. The arrangement is not to everyone's taste, however, some dubbing those rear cans 'wheelbarrow handles'.

Specifications

Engine	Fuel-injected, 16-valve transverse four
Chassis	Aluminum beam frame
Displacement	998cc
Maximum power	175bhp
Maximum torque	78.9lb/ft
Transmission	Six gears
St 1/4 mile	10.58 seconds
Terminal speed	146.8mph
Maximum speed	178.2mph
Brakes, front	2 x 300mm discs, four-piston calipers
Brakes, rear	220mm disc, single-piston caliper
Suspension, front	43mm inverted forks, fully adjustable
Suspension, rear	Monoshock, fully adjustable
Dry weight	175kg/386lbs
Wheelbase	1,390mm/54.7in
Fuel capacity	17litres/4.5 USgallons
Seat height	825mm/32.5in
Tyres, front	120/70 x 17
Tyres, rear	190/55 x 17
Price	£8,799/US$11,199

The new ZX-10R is arguably the fastest, most potent superbike ever built

A no-holds-barred successor to the ZZ-R1100 has been a long time coming but, boy, was it worth the wait...

Japanese motorcycling giant Kawasaki has a long, glorious history of powerhouse superbikes dating way back to the Z1 of 1973. The all-new ZZ-R1400 (ZX14 in the United States) continues that tradition, and then some.

Following in the hallowed footsteps of legendary speed machines such as the GPz900R of 1983, the ZZ-R1100 of 1990 and the more recent ZX-10, the 1400 boasts a claimed 187.7bhp from its

Kawasaki ZZ-R1400

four-cylinder engine and a top speed approaching 200mph. In short, it has everything it takes to warp-thrust it back to the top of the super-speed tree.

But if all that conjures up images of a fire-breathing beast to ride, think again – the ZZ-R1400 is an all-round agreeable sports tourer, too. Its power delivery is astonishingly smooth, its handling nimble yet assured and it has a

seamless spread of both power and torque. It doesn't end there, either. The ZZ-R1400's clutch is light and crisp, the riding position decently low and narrow and, with the entire machine's centre of gravity also low, the big Kawasaki is also impressively manageable both around town and at speed. In all, its handling is outstanding – far greater than the its own Kawasaki stablemate, the ZZ-R1200, and as good as, if not better, than the ZX-12R.

But ultimately, with the ZZ-R1400, it's all about speed. And what speed there is! Wind the twist grip hard and as soon as the tachometer reaches 6,000rpm the monstrous Kawasaki explodes into warp drive. There's enough power available to cause sheer mayhem should the mood take you. What's more, with excellent aerodynamics (including a depression on the top of the fuel tank enabling the rider to tuck in from the wind) this speed is comfortable, too.

And that's not the only time it's comfortable. The ZZ-R1400's riding position is very relaxed and the rider doesn't get cramped. The handlebars are positioned so as to not create undue stress on the wrist and elbows, and the screen – while a bit low at a relaxed pace – manages to keep most of the bug-filled air off the throat.

Overall, even ignoring for a moment the astonishing performance potential, there's a lot to lust over with the ZZ-R1400 – dial in the speed quotient as well and it's a truly awesome machine. It's the fastest accelerating machine in its class, has the handling to match and there's more power on tap than you can shake a stick at. The new ZZR may not have moved the world on technically, but use the throttle as it was designed to be used, and you'll find the bike can move like nothing else. Welcome back Kawasaki ZZR.

Fastest or not?

The ZZ-R1400 may now be the world's fastest production machine, with a top speed of 189mph, but it hasn't come easily or without dispute. Japanese superbikes are now subject to a 'gentleman's agreement' that caps top speed at 300kph (186mph). The ZZ-R only beat that speed when the electronic restrictor was bypassed. Pre-agreement Busas, meanwhile, posted speeds of up to 193mph. So which is fastest? The debate continues…

Vents

The massive, Ferrari Testarossa-style fairing side vents are there for much more than just style. They play a significant part in the ZZ-R1400's cooling requirements, aiding the flow of air through its massive radiator, and also are a major factor in the bike's all-important aerodynamics.

Lights

The very latest 'projector beam' technology is used in the ZZ-R1400's headlights, whereby strong lenses focus the units' beams. This enables them to be not only more powerful, but also smaller and less cumbersome – a factor which, again, only serves to aid the machine's aerodynamics.

Faster still?

In the United States one of the very first production ZZ-R1400's went to drag-racing champion Ricky Gadsen, who promptly modified his machine and proved it could go faster still, posting a sub-10-second standing quarter mile time with just an extended swing arm, power pipe and racing wheels and tyres.

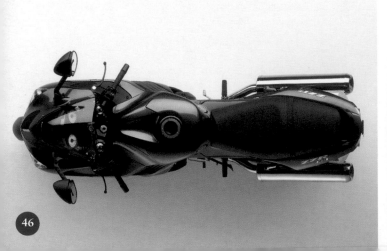

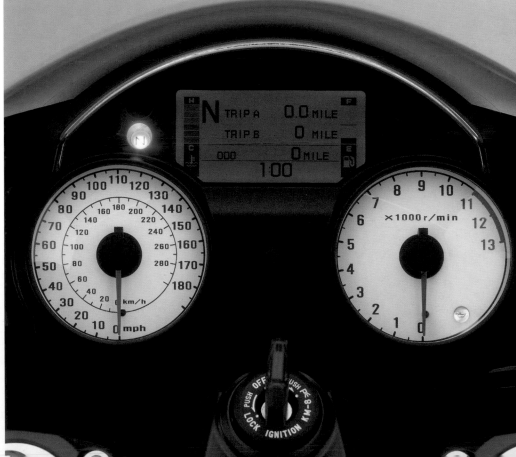

Specifications

Engine	Fuel-injected, 16-valve transverse four
Chassis	Aluminum twin spar
Displacement	1,352cc
Maximum power	187bhp
Maximum torque	113.5lb/ft
Transmission	Six gears
St 1/4 mile	10.25 seconds
Terminal speed	142.03mph
Maximum speed	189.20mph
Brakes, front	2 x 310mm discs, four-piston calipers
Brakes, rear	250 disc, twin-piston calipers
Suspension, front	43mm inverted forks, fully adjustable
Suspension, rear	Monoshock, fully adjustable
Dry weight	215kg/474lbs
Wheelbase	1,460mm/57.5in
Fuel capacity	22ltr/5.8 US gallons
Seat height	800mm/31.5in
Tyres, front	120/70 x 17
Tyres, rear	190/50 x 17
Price	£8,995/US$11,499

*There's enough power available
to cause sheer mayhem should
the mood take you...*

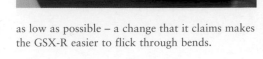

Suzuki set a cat among the pigeons when it unleashed the very first GSX-R1000 at the turn of the millennium. The latest model is more like a tiger...

Just like the 1992 Honda FireBlade, the first R1 and the original GSX-R1000, the GSX-R1000 K5 rocked the superbike world when it was launched in 2005.

The new GSX-R not only boasted the most radical styling in the class, it was a new machine from the ground up: the frame was all new, the engine was reworked with a capacity boosted from 989cc to 999cc and, of course, there was

Suzuki GSX-R1000 K5/6

that radical new, MotoGP-style exhaust. This resulted in brake horsepower measurement of 175, as claimed by Suzuki. Although rival bikes may have appeared to come close to this, in tests the Suzuki would likely have come out on top, as the firm tends to be more accurate regarding the claims made.

The all-new chassis was designed to bring as much weight as possible into the middle of the bike. But Suzuki had also decided to move the bike's weight down, making the center of gravity

as low as possible – a change that it claims makes the GSX-R easier to flick through bends.

Engine changes were comprehensive, too. The reduced weight of the engine's internal parts meant it could rev higher, with the redline now at 13,750rpm. In the fuel-injection system two fuel injectors per cylinder were now used: one operating all the time, the other cutting in to give an extra blast of fuel at high revs and big throttle openings. A bigger bore meant that new larger, but lighter, pistons were used.

Overall, so many items were changed that few parts from the old version fitted the 2005 machine. In short, every characteristic the class holds dear was reclaimed and rewritten by the big Suzuki. It was more powerful, lighter, was easier to ride, had better handling and was even cheaper than its rivals. Is it any wonder, therefore, that it was an instant and unmitigated success?

This year's K6 model remains unchanged from the K5 bar some new color schemes. But even though the competition has caught up slightly (they've all dropped their prices, the ZX-10R is ultimately faster, the Blade sharper and the R1 is closer on power) but the GSX-R1000 is still a superbike of epic proportions.

The Suzuki has the longest stroke motor of all the 1,000s and, weighing in at 166kg, is by far the lightest. These two factors conspire to deliver breathtaking acceleration at low rpm and ultimately searing top speed. In addition, it's all done to the accompaniment of a hollow, metallic roar that is simply electrifying.

But that is not the end of the story. The big GSX-R is also as good at mashing up the racetrack as it is at pottering around on the road thanks to its plush suspension and grunty motor. The Suzuki is far more usable on the road than its rivals from Yamaha and Kawasaki and, if it has to give way to the latest Fireblade thanks to the Honda's sharper chassis, crisper handling and all-round user-friendliness, then that's only just the case.

A winner on both road and track

The GSX-R1000K5/6 has proved to be one of the world's most successful ever production racers in only its second year of production. Not only is it the reigning world superbike champion in the hands of Australian Troy Corser, it's also the reigning AMA Superbike champion (via Mat Mladin). Plus it's won innumerable national and endurance championships.

Machine of the year

The GSX-R's success can be measured in ways other than pure performance or racetrack success. The big Suzuki was also voted Machine of the Year by countless motorcycling magazines worldwide.

It's all in the genes

In terms of performance and sheer ability the latest GSX-R1000 may be a world away from the machine that started it all for Suzuki, the 1985 GSX-R750, but there's no doubting the two are related. Sure, the original's oil-cooling and box-section cradle frame have been replaced by watercooling and a twin spar chassis, but the whole ethos – ultra-light weight and screaming power – remains unchanged.

Less is more

The latest GSX-R's front brake calipers may be only four-piston (compared with the original's massive six-piston items) but they are actually even more powerful due to the latest 'radial mount' technology.

Specifications

Engine	Fuel-injected, 16-valve transverse four
Chassis	Aluminum beam frame
Displacement	999cc
Maximum power	176bhp
Maximum torque	87lb/ft
Transmission	Six gears
St 1/4 mile	10.24 seconds
Terminal speed	145.73mph
Maximum speed	180.7mph
Brakes, front	2 x 310mm discs, four-piston calipers
Brakes, rear	220 disc, two-piston caliper
Suspension, front	43mm inverted forks, fully adjustable
Suspension, rear	Monoshock, fully adjustable
Dry weight	166kg/366lbs
Wheelbase	1,405mm/55.3in
Fuel capacity	18ltr/4.7 US gall
Seat height	810mm/31.9in
Tyres, front	120/70 x 17
Tyres, rear	190/50 x 17
Price	£8,799/US$10,999

*Every characteristic the
class holds dear was reclaimed
and rewritten by the big Suzuki*

In the superbike age there have been many kings of speed, but there has only been one Hayabusa

Few bikes have ever been so focused. Fewer still have been so successful in achieving such a goal that they have remained at the top of their game for years. The machine here is Suzuki's immense GSX1300R Hayabusa. Its claim to fame? Simple – being the world's fastest motorcycle.

Suzuki set about its 200mph target with a double-pronged attack. A glance at the big GSX gives a hint at the first approach – radical

Suzuki GSX1300R Hayabusa

aerodynamics that culminate in swoopy bodywork that looks like nothing else on the road.

The second, however, was the hammer blow: a massive 1,300cc tranverse four cylinder powerplant capable of delivering more power than ever achieved before by a production motorcycle. Back in 1999, Suzuki's claimed 175bhp was simply awesome.

For the first time, a motorcycle's styling was less the work of a designer's pen, and much more the results of extensive wind tunnel testing. A narrow, smooth nose was crucial – hence the use of stacked twin headlights and faired-in indicators – while a hump-backed tail unit was imperative for drag reduction.

But that striking profile is only one half of the GSX1300R recipe. The Busa's engine is also more than merely power-packed. A huge peak torque figure of 102lbs/ft reveals a level of sheer grunt that gives the Suzuki easy, yet explosive, power, whatever speed and whatever gear you're in. Even, say, in top gear at just 1500rpm, the powerful Hayabusa pulls away effortlessly.

But if the Busa's technology was the dawn of a new era, riders required a whole new approach as well. It's not that the Suzuki's difficult to ride though – far from it.

A potential monster the Busa may be, but when you're not in the mood for big speed, it's an easily manageable pussycat. Yet when you do turn up the power – watch out, the Hayabusa accelerates so rapidly and relentlessly, you'll need to rethink everything you know about performance.

All this paints the Busa as something of a one trick pony, focused entirely on straightline speed. But that would be hugely unfair because there is much more to the Suzuki than just monumental power.

The massively strong twin spar aluminum frame imbues it with far more ability and agility through the turns than you might expect, and the fact that all its bulk is carried low makes it stable and predictable, too.

If ultimate speed is your bag then the Hayabusa is still probably the one to go for. But it's a decent all-round motorcycle, too.

New ones are slower

The original Suzuki Hayabusa of 1999 posted top speeds in the low 190mph zone. This was at a time when the machine itself was the full, unemasculated 175bhp version and before the latest pinpoint accuracy of satellite data logger timing equipment. The latest versions are now subject to a 'gentleman's agreement' restriction of 300kph (or 186mph), so can't match that figure.

What's in a name?

In the Hayabusa's case, a bird. Or, to be strictly accurate, a revered Japanese hunting bird of prey, which is where the GSX1300R gets its more popular moniker...

Cult following

Such is the reverence, respect even, in which the Hayabusa has been held by a significant section of the motorcycling fraternity, that it's developed something of a cult following the world over, but particularly in the United States and the UK.

Size isn't everything

The Hayabusa may boast 1,300ccs and monstrous performance but, in many ways, it's physically quite small. Although fairly long, the weight is all carried low and the seat height is manageable for virtually everyone – something that certainly can't be said of the very latest 1,000cc sportsbikes.

Substance over style

Although unusually styled, the engineering behind the Hayabusa was conventional. It has an across-the-frame four-cylinder engine and a twin-spar alloy beam frame, but the strange looks are a unique consequence of the quest for improved aerodynamics.

Specifications

Engine	Fuel-injected, 16-valve transverse four
Chassis	Aluminum twin spar
Displacement	1,298cc
Maximum power	175bhp
Maximum torque	103lb/ft
Transmission	Six gears
St 1/4 mile	10.29 seconds
Terminal speed	141.56mph
Maximum speed	181.40mph
Brakes, front	2 x 320mm front discs with six-piston calipers
Brakes, rear	240mm rear disc with two-piston caliper
Suspension, front	43mm inverted forks, fully adjustable
Suspension, rear	Single rear shock, fully adjustable
Dry weight	217kg/478lbs
Wheelbase	1,485mm/58.5in
Fuel capacity	21ltr/5.5 US gall
Seat height	805mm/31.6in
Tyres, front	120/70 x 17
Tyres, rear	190/50 x 17
Price	£8,649/US$11,099

*When you do turn up the power –
watch out because the Hayabusa
accelerates so rapidly and relentlessly,
you'll need to rethink everything you
know about performance*

The original R1 of 1998 rewrote the superbike rules. The latest is the very pinnacle of the art

Yamaha's 2004 R1, boasting 180bhp and just 172kg was the first mass production superbike to crest the milestone of managing to produce 1bhp per kilogram.

Outwardly, thanks to its family signature 'fox eye' headlamps, that machine seemed to be little more than the latest derivation of the R-series liter-class bike. But that façade hid a wealth of

Yamaha YZF1000R1

changes under the skin which had little in common with any previous machine.

Its tech spec alone seemed more like that of a GP racer. In the first instance, its characteristic five valves per cylinder transverse four powerplant was all-new and boasted a massive peak

horsepower figure of 172bhp, rising to a gob-smacking 180bhp when its ram-air system (the first time it had been used on the R1) started to work at speed. The way that the motor was held, and the chassis layout itself, bore direct comparison with Yamaha's barnstorming 990cc M1 MotoGP machine.

The 2006 R1 is faster still. Granted, the very latest machine doesn't look much different to its 2004 sibling apart from the paint scheme but there are a plethora of improvements that have the culmulative effect of returning the Yamaha back to the very top of the superbike tree.

First up, peak claimed horsepower is boosted once again – up to 175bhp from 172. The chassis is different, too. The distinctive twin spar aluminum Deltabox frame has been refined with excess metal removed from a number of areas to not just shed weight but to also introduce a degree of 'flex' aimed at improving rider feel. The swingarm is longer (by 20mm) and wider with the aim of both aiding traction from the rear wheel and enabling the latest generation of superwide (190-200mm) sports tyres to fit without touching. Finally, the suspension units front and rear have been recalibrated to improve handling.

The big Yamaha is still every inch an R1. Like previous examples it thrives on revs, requiring its neck (and twistgrip) to be thoroughly wrung to get the most from it thanks to its short-stroke engine layout and inherent hunger for revs. In short, you have to ride it and rev it like you would a smaller capacity machine, but when you do, you're rewarded in spades.

That said, the R1 has a tamer side, too. It has always been intended to be a machine with road, not just track, ability and as such its ergonomics and suspension settings are far more comfortable than most of its rivals. At the end of the day, the latest R1 may still struggle to better its rivals in the rarefied confines of the race track. But where it matters – on the road – not much comes close.

Now there's better still...

The R1 isn't the only Yamaha superbike available in 2006. The Japanese firm has also made available a special limited edition version dubbed the LE in the United States and SP in Europe. The bike boasts racing specification Ohlins forks and rear suspension and lightweight Marchesini wheels.

Replica colors

A special 'retro' color scheme was also launched for the R1 in 2006. The yellow and black 'speed block' scheme replicates Yamaha USA's racing colors, as made famous worldwide by legendary racer Kenny Roberts.

Racers ride them too

American MotoGP star Colin Edwards was involved in both the development and launch of the latest R1. The 'Texas Tornado', bedecked in matching yellow and black retro leathers and helmet, rode the 'speed block' R1 and R1 LE at the world press debut of the bike.

Get ready to shift gear

The latest R1, like a growing number of modern superbikes, employs a 'gearchange light' on its instrument display. When the engine hits peak revs (just before the redline), the light comes on to indicate when to shift gear.

Specifications

Engine	Fuel-injected, 20-valve transverse four
Chassis	Aluminum twin-beam frame
Displacement	998cc
Maximum power	175bhp
Maximum torque	78.6lb/ft
Transmission	Six gears
St 1/4 mile	10.54 seconds
Terminal speed	144.59mph
Maximum speed	176mph
Brakes, front	2 x 320mm discs, four-piston calipers
Brakes, rear	220mm disc, two-piston caliper
Suspension, front	43mm inverted forks, fully adjustable
Suspension, rear	Monoshock, fully adjustable
Dry weight	173kg/381lbs
Wheelbase	1,415mm/55.7in
Fuel capacity	18ltr/4.7 US gall
Seat height	835mm/32.8in
Tyres, front	120/70 x 17
Tyres, rear	190/50 x 17
Price	£8,799/US$11,299

There's a raft of subtle technical changes that catapult the latest R1 to the very top of the superbike class

Aprilia may not be the most famous of Italian superbike manufacturers but its latest RSV1000R Factory is probably the best

Aprilia is the new kid on the block when it comes to Italian superbikes. But what the Noale, near Venice, firm lacks in terms of heritage, compared to the likes of Moto Guzzi, Ducati and MV Agusta, it more than makes up for in cutting edge technology and 21st century sporting prowess.

Its flagship superbike is the 60-degree V-twin powered RSV Mille. Launched originally in 1998, the big vee impressed the motorcycling world by

Aprilia RSV1000R Factory

managing to successfully blend classic Italian V-twin charisma with Japanese performance, reliability and build quality. The fact that it came in at a price midway between similar Japanese and Italian machinery was the icing on the cake.

The RSV range received a complete overhaul in 2004, with all-new styling being the biggest giveaway. That bike was updated again in 2006. And although the 2006 Mille might, at first glance, seem very similar to the 2004 model, Aprilia has altered almost every fairing panel and made some significant upgrades to the engine and the chassis.

As in the past, two versions are on offer. The base model is the RSV-R. But it's the top of the range version, RSV-R Factory that has biking aficionados drooling the world over.

Both versions share exactly the same engine, now with revised cylinder heads and a new management system to help boost power to 143bhp, up from the previous model's 137bhp.

Peak power comes at 10,000rpm, but despite the engine's revvy nature it's not short of torque, hitting 76lb/ft at 8,000rpm. A more aerodynamically efficient ram air intake helps add 3% more power at high speed, theoretically giving the bike about 147bhp when going at full chat.

But it's the two model's rolling chassis which set them apart and which make the Factory the motorcycling jewel it truly is.

The Factory is the track-ready version of the 1000R and has the extra details needed for circuit mastery – top notch Ohlins suspension front and rear, an Ohlins steering damper, and very light OZ forged wheels (those of the R, while the same style, are cast aluminum and heavier). These differences are the sort of stuff we all dream of getting in our Christmas sacks.

The most visible difference between the two is in the color detailing. The 1000R gets a dark-coated frame and is very nondescript. The Factory has a bling golden sheen, golden wheels and another gold finish on the nitride-coated Ohlins stanchions and sliders.

And this pot of gold is good value, too – it'd set you back at least £2,300/$4,200 to buy the Ohlins suspension and OZ race-ready wheels alone. And Ducati wonders why Aprilia always comes out on top in comparative tests?

Steady goes it

Aprilia have tuned out the old RSV's light and sometimes twitchy front end feel by kicking out the steering head angle by one degree to increase trail from 100mm to 101.7mm. Fast and hard pulls on the bars don't upset it even when running deep into turns on the brakes.

Feel the quality

Quality components rule on the RSV – from the Brembo radially mounted calipers and braided steel brake lines to the transparent taillight and indicator lenses. Even the headlight has come under revision to leave red blobs floating in your vision if stared at in daytime. The four faired-in beams now consist of dual main and low bulbs so no more 'one-eyed' stares from the front, and the end of helpful people asking if you knew one of the bulbs had blown...

Slimline tonic

Bodywork has been slimmed and sharpened, and now incorporates larger side vents to help suck out engine heat. The side panels are now two-piece units instead of the intricate 1000-piece puzzle of before. A new aerodynamic screen doesn't do much for the rider but this depends on how tall you are. For anyone above 5ft 10in and with mileage in mind, you'd be wise to invest in an aftermarket double-bubble screen – the only piece of kit needed to keep life bearable as there's enough room and a civilized riding position to keep even giants happy.

Masterbike 2006

The RSV Factory was the surprise victor of the massively influential and prestigious 2006 international 'Masterbike' competition when the best superbikes battle head-to-head around a racetrack. The testers were 20 of the world's leading motorcycle magazines. The circuit was the Grand Prix track at Jerez in southern Spain.

A new era

After a number of years of financial insecurity, Aprilia is now part of the massive Italian Piaggio motorcycling and scooter conglomerate (as also is, as part of the same deal, Moto Guzzi). As a result, significant investment is once again being made, production is back on track, and a raft of new models are under development including, rumor has it, an all-new V4-powered superbike due before the end of the decade.

Specifications

Engine	Fuel-injected, DOHC 60-degree V-twin
Chassis	Aluminum twin spar frame
Displacement	998cc
Maximum power	143bhp
Maximum torque	75lb/ft
Transmission	Six gears
Standing quarter mile	11.3 seconds
Terminal speed	137mph
Maximum speed	167mph
Brakes, front	2 x 320mm discs, four-piston calipers
Brakes, rear	220mm disc, twin-piston caliper
Suspension, front	43 mm Ohlins titanium nitride (TiN) coated inverted forks, fully adjustable
Suspension, rear	Monoshock, fully adjustable
Dry weight	185kg/408lbs
Wheelbase	1418mm/55.8in
Fuel capacity	18ltr/4.75 US gall
Seat height	810mm/31.9in
Tyres, front	120/70 x 17
Tyres, rear	190/50 x 17
Price	£10,349/US$17,999

A sleeping Italian giant returns. Benelli, one of the Grand Prix greats of the 1950s, is back with a superbike capable of mixing with the best

Along with Moto Guzzi, Ducati and Laverda, Benelli is one of the great names of Italian motorcycling. Its history in the last decade has been anything but smooth, but its flagship machine, the Tornado, remains a superbike truly worthy of the name and is an icon of Italian motorcycling.

The first Tornado was launched in 2000 and from every angle of its sculpted form, it was an Italian masterpiece. Powered by a state-of-the-art

Benelli Tornado Tre 1130

liquid-cooled, fuel-injected transverse triple, it originally displaced 900cc. For 2006, however, Benelli has increased its capacity and boosted performance to create the Tornado 1130.

Like with so many superbikes before, the Tornado is majestic even at standstill. Quality and class drips from every pore. The suspension is some of the very best available, race-spec stoppers are provided by Brembo, the wheels are equally exotic forged alloy Marchesinis and the bodywork is fashioned from crisp, expensive carbon fiber. All that goes without mentioning

the unique and delicious twin underseat fans which are there to draw heat away from the underseat radiator.

Then, if you were not already convinced, once you thumb the Benelli's starter for the first time you'll be utterly infatuated.

That three-cylinder 1,130cc engine is a breath of fresh air compared to a homogenised Japanese four. It's busting at the seams with ground-churning low and mid-range power, and with 97lb/ft of torque and 161bhp at the crank it's finally got the power worthy of its name. You can be as lazy as you want with the gearbox – just twist the throttle and, whoosh, you're a dot in the distance.

As speeds rise, the Benelli gets better yet: the race-bike firm suspension becomes more supple, the brakes become more tactile, and you can start taking advantage of the Tornado's impeccable stability through fast sweeping corners.

It's not perfect, of course. Because it's so stiffly set-up, the Tornado is very fatiguing to ride any distance.

What's more, the clutch is heavy, the seat is far too thinly padded and, at just less than 195kg, the Tornado is neither particularly light nor small. Nor can it match the latest from Japan in terms of pure performance.

Instead you have to compare the Benelli with its fellow Italian superbike rivals. From a performance point of view, it's on par with a Ducati 999 or an Aprilia RSV, but because it has one more cylinder than the twins, it's livelier and arguably more involving to ride – it howls rather than roars.

If you're a fan of exotic Italian superbikes, lust after the sound of triples and love the styling, there are few better bikes than the Tornado 1130.

The Chinese connection

Benelli's plant may still be in Pesaro, but as of 18 months ago or so, Benelli is a Chinese-owned company. Following financial difficulties Benelli was put up for sale by the Merlonis and was wholly purchased by the Qianjiang Group Co. Ltd, China's largest motorcycle manufacturer..

The difference a three makes

At 185kg (407lb), it's no flyweight. But if you imagine that the leading lightweight four-cylinder machine is Suzuki's blistering GSX-R1000 at 170kg (375lb) and the leading twins like Ducati's new superbike 999 at 199kg (437.8lb), then the Tornado is the perfect balance of the three configurations in terms of power, poise and performance.

Green is the color…

The Tornado's most prominent color way is grccn and silver, a modern day take on the firm's racing colors back in its 1950s heyday. Of course, yellow, red or black alternatives are available.

Specifications

Engine	Liquid-cooled, 12v, DOHC, in-line-triple. Fuel injection
Chassis	Tubular steel trellis/cast aluminum mix frame
Displacement	1,130cc
Maximum power	161bhp
Maximum torque	97lb/ft
Transmission	Six gears
Standing quarter mile	11.3 seconds
Terminal speed	132mph
Maximum speed	164mph
Brakes, front	Brembo, 2 x 320mm front discs with four-piston radially mounted calipers
Brakes, rear	240mm rear disc with four-piston caliper
Suspension, front	50mm Marzocchi upside down forks, fully adjustable
Suspension, rear	Single rear Extreme Technology shock, fully adjustable (with high and low speed compression damping)
Dry weight	195kg/430lbs
Wheelbase	1419mm/55.9in
Fuel capacity	21ltr/5.5 US gall
Seat height	810mm/31.9in
Tyres, front	120/70 x 17
Tyres, rear	190/55 x 17
Price	£9,999/not on sale in the US

Take advantage
impeccable
fast-

Bimota is back. The Italian firm that created the most desirable machines in the world in the 1970s and 80s by blending Japanese engines with bespoke chassis, is now back for more

Long the 'enfant terrible' of the Italian motorcycle industry, Bimota was formed in 1973 and headed by Massimo Tamburini (later the designer of Ducati's iconic 916 and the MV Agusta F4 and Brutale). It made its name by building exquisitely made, fine-handling motorcycles using powerful engines from the likes of Suzuki and Yamaha. This was all at a time when Japanese engines were way ahead of their chassis technology, so Bimotas made sense and we all lusted over them.

Bimota
DB5

More recently, however, as mass-produced bikes became better, Bimota's appeal lessened. But now Bimota is back, with new owners and new investors. The DB5 is the first bike to come out of this new set-up, and although Bimota remains tight-lipped about what's next, expect its next new bikes to be far more performance orientated. In the flesh, there's no doubting that this Italian piece of gorgeousness is 100% pure sportsbike. With its Ohlins suspension, Brembo radial-mount

brakes, a track-focused riding position, a small thin plank for a seat and no room for a pillion, this isn't a touring machine. Its prime objective is to scorch through corners and, being a Bimota, look gorgeous while doing so.

The DB5 is also like nothing ever seen before. It's incredibly thin (barely wider than its slimline 992cc Ducati V-twin power plant), and the hand-made, tubular steel trellis space frame makes the little Bimota seem even more slender than it really is.

The attention to detail is simply stunning. The side stand has exquisite cut-out slots, keeping weight to a minimum. And in true Bimota style of yore, there are beautifully-machined slices of aircraft-grade billet aluminum everywhere: the chunky top and bottom yokes, the lateral plates on the frame and swingarm, and the brackets holding the Brembo radial mount front brake calipers to the bottom of the titanium-nitride coated Ohlins forks.

The air-cooled Ducati engine was chosen for its lightness and its elegant simplicity; with a claimed crank figure of just 92bhp, performance isn't exactly arm-wrenching. But the unit has none of the ugly plumbing and wiring of, say, Ducati's more powerful water-cooled 999 sister and so suits the design of the DB5 better.

This engine is all about torque. It rewards you if you keep it in the higher gears and let the motor's grunt fling you out of the corners. Unlike a more highly tuned motor, you won't disappear in a flurry of revs with a rocket up your rear end.

With its Ohlins suspension, waif-like 156kg dry weight, and easy-going power delivery, handling is race bike-like impressive. Corners are what the DB5 is all about.

There's no doubt that £17,000 ($39,800) is a lot of money for a bike, especially for one that can't match even the latest Japanese 600s for pure engine performance. Any Japanese sportsbike would be a lot faster, and for less you could own of the most gorgeous, best-handling and exciting Ducatis ever built: the 749R. What you're paying for here though is inimitable style, quality and exclusivity.

There's slim and there's...

Although the radial-mount Brembos brakes do the job of scrubbing off speed with little fuss, it's not so easy to actually hang on. Although the narrow, sloped tank looks the business, it's hard to grip with knees and stop yourself sliding up the tank, so it's quite an effort to brace yourself with arms in full anchors-out mode.

Fine tuning

Push the pace and the DB5 gets a bit heavy to steer, especially through fast chicanes, but since the Ohlins rear shock has a ride height adjuster, it should be easy to 'jack' the bike up to suit you and make its steering quicker if it's a problem. It's just one of the bonuses that demonstrates the massive level of adjustment offered by the superb Ohlins suspension.

More than just a pretty face

Although the Ducati motor has Ducati fuel injection, it's controlled by Bimota's own engine management system (they're not able to use the same supplier Ducati uses). Credit to Bimota then that the throttle response is smooth throughout the rev range and is especially impressive from a closed throttle at low revs.

A mirror mire

Those big antler-like mirrors, which dominate the front of the bike, are actually monumentally useless.

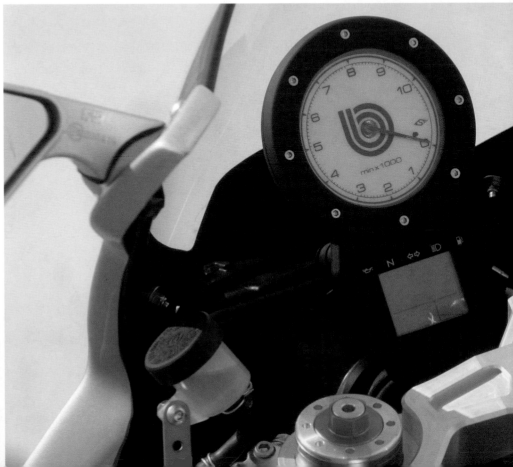

Specifications

Engine	Air cooled, four stroke, 90° V-twin, SOHC, desmodromic two valves per cylinder
Chassis	Tubular chrome molybdenum steel trellis with lateral plates in aircraft alloy
Displacement	992cc
Maximum power	92bhp
Maximum torque	61lb/ft
Transmission	Six gears
Standing quarter mile	11.9 seconds
Terminal speed	123mph
Maximum speed	130mph
Brakes, front	2 x 298mm discs, four-piston calipers
Brakes, rear	220mm disc, two-piston calipers
Suspension, front	Ohlins upside-down fully adjustable forks with TiN surface treatment
Suspension, rear	Fully adjustable Ohlins monoshock
Dry weight	156kg/344lbs
Wheelbase	1425mm/56.1in
Fuel capacity	17ltr/4.49 US gall
Seat height	790mm/31.1in
Tyres, front	120/90 x 17
Tyres, rear	180/55 x 17
Price	£17,000/US$39,800

The bike's prime objective is to scorch through corners and, being a Bimota, look gorgeous while doing so

For a long time BMW motorcycles have been synonymous with sensible, staid tourers where the emphasis is on effectiveness rather than exhilaration. Not any more...

The K1200S was BMW's first real modern superbike. And when it came to technical innovation, the BMW found itself the king of the hill on the superbike's release in 2005.

Radical design and superlative engineering were to be found wherever you looked. At the front, BMW did away with the decades-old telescopic fork and used a wishbone arrangement with a single shock. At the rear, BMW's traditional shaft drive was mated to its patented Paralever rising rate monoshock.

BMW K1200S

The all-new, longitudinally-mounted four cylinder engine boasts 165bhp with 96lb/ft of torque, enough to catapult the 1200S from 0 to 62mph in 2.8 seconds. Yet when you thumb the starter, the 16-valve in-line four-cylinder powerplant comes to life with a non-threatening purr.

At slow speeds the K1200S's sheer size shows. This is no tiny lightweight after all. It scales in at 565lbs with its five-gallon fuel tank topped off. And, with a wheelbase that's 61.9 inches long, it is over six inches longer than most of its sportier, more nimble competition.

But once up to speed, all thoughts of this BMW being large and lardy are cancelled out by the supreme comfort and complete control that it offers. In a straight line, the S is smooth and steady, soaking up road imperfections without complaint.

The horizon rushes towards you as fast as the the K's tacho needle rips up to redline. And if you keep it spinning hard as you click up through the six-speed gearbox with the throttle against the stop, you'll experience the uncensored adrenaline rush of BMW's best ever sportsbike.

It's no wallflower either. Keep the throttle pinned and the note from the four-into-one stainless exhaust system morphs from a growl into a full-bore rasping wail.

Overall, the Beemer is an astonishing piece of kit. It may not have the raw powerhouse appeal of some of its rivals, but it still boasts over 160bhp and manages to lay them down on the road in a far more effective, useful, versatile and yet still exhilarating way than almost any other machine can match.

Its ride is creamy smooth and you always feel in control. Couple this with the best in BMW technology that towers over the competition and you have a staggering sport-tourer. Yes, you lose some of the top end performance offered by other bikes but you make up for it in comfort. Convinced? You should be – we recommend taking one out for a whirl as soon as possible.

Electronic Suspension Adjustment (ESA)

With this option, there are three different riding choices available: single rider, rider with luggage, or rider with pillion and luggage. In typical BMW fashion though, that's not all the ESA does. You can also alter the suspension setting depending on how you're going to be riding the Beemer. There's Normal, Comfort and Sport. Selecting one adjusts the front rebound plus the compression and rebound at the rear.

This Bayern motor works

The all-new longitudinally mounted four offers everything a sports rider could wish for. The cylinder bank is tilted forward by 55°, while the center of gravity is very low due to the engine's extremely narrow width. Its leaning angle and ergonomics are also excellent. The engine's power turns to precision in the newly designed six-speed gearbox.

Slick Shifter

The BMW features a creamy and spot-on close-ratio six-speed transmission that lets the rider make the most of the engine sitting below them.

Specifications

Engine:	Fuel-injected, 16-valve longitudinal four
Chassis	Aluminum with engine as stressed member
Displacement	1,157cc
Maximum power	165bhp
Maximum torque	96lb/ft
Transmission	Six gears, shaft drive
Standing quarter mile	11.75 seconds
Terminal speed	130mph
Maximum speed	178.3mph
Brakes, front	2 x 320mm discs, four-piston calipers. Optional ABS
Brakes, rear	265mm disc, two-piston caliper. Optional ABS
Suspension, front	BMW Motorrad Duolever front suspension with single spring adjustable for rebound damping, optional Electronic Suspension Adjustment (ESA)
Suspension, rear	Monoshock, fully adjustable, optional Electronic Suspension Adjustment (ESA)
Dry weight	176kg/388lbs
Wheelbase	1571mm/61.9in
Fuel capacity	19ltr/5.02US gall
Seat height	820mm/32.3in
Tyres, front	120/70 x 17
Tyres, rear	190/50 x 17
Price	£10,100 (£10,895 with ABS)/ US$17,585 ($17,985)

In a straight line, the S is smooth and steady, soaking up road imperfections without complaint

After the World Superbike Championship-dominating 916 of the 1990s, the 999 had a lot to live up to. But the R version does that, and then some...

There's probably never been a tougher superbike act to follow than that of Ducati's iconic 916. The Massimo Tamburini-penned (of Bimota fame) beauty of 1994 not only catapulted Ducati right to the top of the superbike tree but it went on to dominate the World Superbike Championship for the remainder of the decade, mostly in the hands of Brit Carl Fogarty. The fact that the 916 was also a Ducati, red, and powered by arguably the best V-twin (the liquid-cooled, four-valve

Ducati 999R

'Desmoquattro') motor ever engineered, ensured the 916's iconic status for years to come.

Unfortunately, and despite numerous updates over time (rising first from 916 to 996 and then 998ccs), those years eventually had to come to an end. And when they did in 2002, the Pierre Terblanche-designed 999 was rolled out as the 916's successor.

By contrast, and perhaps as no great surprise, the 999 has struggled to live up to its illustrious predecessor. Opinion is split on its styling and although indisputably a faster, better handling, more modern machine, most consider the 999 to lack the 'X-factor' that the 916 had in spades. The 'R' version, however, is a different matter entirely.

Three versions of the 999 are offered for the street: the base 999, the higher spec 'S' version complete with more power and Ohlins suspension in place of the stocker's Showa items, and this, the no-holds-barred daddy of them all.

The R is essentially a homologation specially built to qualify for World Superbike racing. It has a single seat, masses of power and torque, top-notch suspension and brakes, lighter swingarm and Marchesini wheels and, with its blood red frame and black wheels, it looks the part, too.

The R received its biggest update yet in 2005 with a new front fairing, new rear swing arm and suspension, not to mention a major engine upgrade resulting in a full (claimed) 150bhp.

The basic dimensions of the Testastretta engine used on the new 999R remain the same as those of the previous version. Bore and stroke remain 104mm x 58.8mm – however, peak power and torque have been greatly increased. Compared to the previous model's 139bhp at 10,000rpm, the new engine produces 150bhp at 9,750rpm. Torque itself has been increased from 108 Nm (11 kgm) at 8,000rpm, to 116.7 Nm (11.9 kgm) at 8,000rpm.

And the result is simply a revelation. Sure, the latest Aprilia RSV Factory may have won the 2006 Masterbike, but only the lower spec 999S took part in that. Derivatives of the 999R won the 2005 British Superbike Championship, not to mention the 2003 and 2004 World Superbikes Championship. The R is not only blisteringly fast, it has the precision, aplomb and sheer class that only that kind of pedigree and that kind of no-expense spared – and don't forget, this is a $30,000 motorcycle – approach can bring.

Forged wheel rims

Compared to castings, it is possible to use thinner sections since the material is distributed evenly throughout the component. The lower weight of the rims not only reduces the suspended masses (which significantly improves suspension performance), but also greatly reduces the gyroscope effect and improves the handling of the bike at high speeds (the bike is more agile when entering curves).

Carbon build up

The headlamp mount and the new mirror mounts are now in magnesium alloy. The fairing scoops, front fairing between the two side pieces, front mudguard, chain guard, silencer heat shield and windshield fairing are all in carbon fiber.

Posh front end

Apart from the exotic Marchesini forged wheels, high tech detailing abounds elsewhere on the R's front end. The front brake calipers are radially mounted to special mounts on a new Ohlins fork, the legs of which are surfaced in TiN for improved sliding. The two legs have modified smaller diameter springs and the spring guide is now in plastic rather than metal. What hasn't changed, but remains equally exotic, is the 999's cam system which allows the steering head angle to be adjusted and thus also the trail (91 through 97mm).

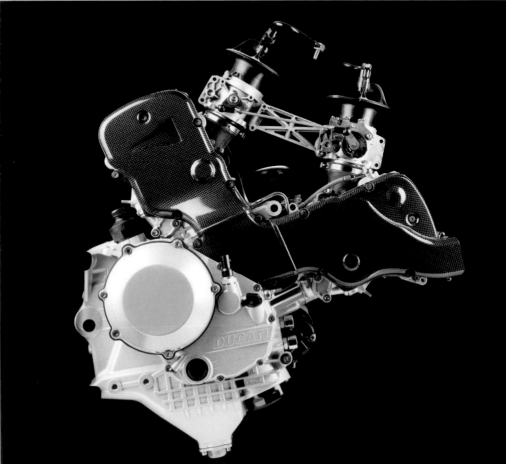

Specifications

Engine	Liquid cooled, four stroke, 90° V-twin, Desmodromic 4 valve per cylinder
Chassis	Steel tubing, trestle-type
Displacement	999cc
Maximum power	150bhp
Maximum torque	86lb/ft
Transmission	Six gears
Standing quarter mile	10.6 seconds
Terminal speed	136mph
Maximum speed	179mph
Brakes, front	2 x 320mm discs, four-piston calipers
Brakes, rear	240mm disc, two-piston caliper
Suspension, front	Ohlins 43mm upside-down fully adjustable fork with TiN surface treatment
Suspension, rear	Progressive linkage with fully adjustable Ohlins monoshock
Dry weight	181kg/399lbs
Wheelbase	1420mm/55.9in
Fuel capacity	15.5ltr/4.1 US gall
Seat height	780mm/30.7in
Tyres, front	120/70 ZR17
Tyres, rear	190/50 ZR17
Price	£19,995/US$29,999

The R is not only blisteringly fast, it has the precision, aplomb and sheer class that only that kind of pedigree and that kind of no-expense spared approach can bring

Say hello to MV's latest, and possibly greatest – the half-F41000S, half-Senna F41000R

When Massimo Tamburini designed the legendary Ducati 916, everyone wondered how its looks could be bettered; the answer came when the man reappeared at MV Agusta. The first result, the F4 750, may have lacked a little in terms of outright performance against the Japanese 1000s, but it more than made up for it in terms of sheer beauty, componentry and perfect craftsmanship.

MV Agusta F4 1000R

The eight years since has seen more variants of the F4 than you can shake a very large stick at. But there's no doubting that each, from 750, to 750S, 1000 and Tamburini, seems to get better than the last. But now, at last, there's one – the new 174bhp F41000R – which has the performance to match its luxury class price tag.

At £14,500 ($26,350), there's no denying that the F41000R is expensive, but it's only £300 ($545) more than the base model F41000S and yet you get an awful lot of goodies for your money.

Firstly the engine has been considerably revised to produce a claimed 174bhp at the crankshaft, 10bhp more than the F4-S (164bhp). It also gets new Magneti Marelli ECU, 50mm Marzocchi forks, Sachs rear shock, exquisite Brembo forged alloy wheels and radial brakes and revised screen.

The sum of all those parts adds up to a sublime package. The engine is faster than all its Japanese equivalents (even if its delivery is a little coarse) while its handling is superior to any ZX-10R, GSX-R and the like. There's a lot of feedback from both tyres, it holds its line through slow or fast turns, it's very stable and the brakes are awesome. Only when being ridden extremely hard is any chassis bugbear highlighted – the 1000R is heavy.

As to whether all of that makes it worth it, it has to be said that both engine and chassis-wise you could get the same levels of performance from any of the MV's Japanese in-line four rivals, whether it's by Honda, Kawasaki, Suzuki or Yamaha.

But then the F41000R is more than just a bike. It is also a thing of extraordinary beauty. Cast a careful eye over those deliciously sculpted flanks, past the four exhaust cans and deep paintwork and look again. The triple-clamp bottom yoke is WSB-spec, the eccentrically adjusted foot pegs and foot levers are F1 quality. Not so obvious is the satin-ally finish on the throttle cable end pipes that makes cadmium plating on Japanese bikes appear cheap and nasty.

Want one? Of course you do...

More power

To eke out an additional 10bhp from the F4 engine, a serious amount of revision work was carried out. The valves are lighter, spaced 2mm longitudinally further apart (the cylinder bores are moved back 1.5mm to allow this) and the intake valve angle has been steepened to let in more inlet charge. Camshafts are also new, with 1mm more lift and, combined with new pistons to suit the new valve arrangement, ensure efficient fuel burn, which means more power. The clutch basket gets strengthened (more basket fingers) and there's one more clutch plate (now ten in total) to deal with the extra bhp.

Less is more...

A total weight of 4.5kg has been sliced from the F4's chassis by reducing the wall thickness on some of the tubular frame's pipework and around the headstock area, as well as fitting forged aluminum Brembo wheels.

Revised suspension

Marzocchi's latest fully adjustable 50mm USD forks are the absolute masters of stiffness and damping action – and so they should be with 13 compression settings and 32 on the rebound side of things. The Sachs rear shock is also fully adjustable and features dual-rate compression damping and hydraulic spring pre-load adjustment.

State-of-the-art brakes

Race-derived Brembo P4/34 front-brake calipers and race-spec pads clamp the larger 320mm discs with enough force and feel to make you wonder whether tyres of a lesser quality than the Pirelli SuperCorsa Pro (fitted as standard) could handle such stopping effect. In answer to why MV Agusta uses a Nissin front master cylinder and not Brembo's own, the answer is simple: MV didn't want its master cylinder to look like that of its competitors and Nissin were able to make one to Tamburini's shapely design.

Specifications

Engine	Liquid-cooled, four-stroke, transverse four cylinder, DOHC, four valves per cylinder
Chassis	Tubular steel Trellis
Displacement	996cc
Maximum power	174bhp
Maximum torque	82lb/ft
Transmission	Six gears
Standing quarter mile	n/a
Terminal speed	n/a
Maximum speed	190mph
Brakes, front	2 x 320mm discs, 320mm front discs with four-piston radial-type calipers
Brakes, rear	210mm rear disc with four-piston caliper
Suspension, front	Marzochi 50mm USD forks, fully adjustable
Suspension, rear	Single Sachs shock, fully adjustable including high- and low-speed compression and rebound-damping
Dry weight	184kg/405lbs
Wheelbase	1,408mm/55.4in
Fuel capacity	21ltr/5.5 US gall
Seat height	810mm/31.8in
Tyres, front	120/70 x 17
Tyres, rear	190/55 x 17
Price	£14,500/US$26,000

A great name, a great reputation and a great road bike... how could the Daytona be anything else but a triumph?

When it comes to motorcycles, the name conjured up most quickly in people's minds is the legendary British marque, Triumph.

The original Triumph Daytona was a 500cc sports twin – little brother to the more revered 650 and, later, the 750 Bonneville, that dates back to the late 1950s and was most popular during the 1960s. At that time, the long-established firm (which was based in Meriden, UK) was one of

Triumph 955i Daytona

motorcycling's world leaders, but it quickly faded, collapsing in the 1970s with the rise to dominance of the Big Four Japanese factories (Honda, Kawasaki, Suzuki, Yamaha).

Today, the Daytona name lives on as the flagship sportsbike of the revived, all-new Triumph concern, now based in Hinckley, UK. Millionaire businessman John Bloor bought the marque in 1983; in 1991 the first all-new products from the brand-new factory hit the road. Among them were two Daytona sportsbikes, a short-lived 750 triple and a 1,000cc four. And, although the bikes that bear the name have changed comprehensively and

repeatedly since then, the Triumph Daytona remains the Hinckley Triumph *par excellence*.

To many, the most significant of the bunch was the 1996 T595 Daytona. Most agree that that bike was the first modern Triumph to truly give the Japanese a run for their money while retaining a characterful, three-cylinder Britishness – but the latest version, the 955i, is the better bike.

Not only is the big Daytona neutral handling and integrated, but it has many admirers and has sold well. It's based on the T595 but boasts improved ground clearance, a revised rear suspension system, new bodywork and a tidier appearance.

In terms of character, the 'Big Brit' is more softly focused than other sportsbikes of similar capacity. The 955cc Triumph is extremely user-friendly, making it ideal for newcomers and experienced riders alike. The power delivery from the flexible big three-cylinder engine is glitch-free, with a smooth feel and a welcome, crisp induction note.

But don't let its softer looks fool you. The 955i handles better than needed – on public roads at least because it's no track weapon. Daytonas aren't seen in large numbers at circuits and this suggests that the majority of buyers prefer riding on the road to racing on the track. And that's exactly where the 955i is most at home.

Triumph went out of its way to ensure the Daytona's suspension was developed and set up with typical roads in mind; this has paid off as the suspension works well. The bike is also comfortable, which is why many are used for touring Continental Europe with a passenger .

And the icing on the cake? The build quality is good, reliability is spot on, and Triumphs hold their value. If you're not swayed by purely the latest and greatest and are looking for a classy, versatile superbike for the road, you won't go far wrong. And if that isn't having your cake and eating it, we don't know what is.

Triumph revival

The name may be historic, but the badge is the only thing modern-day that Triumphs share with their namesakes of old. British building tycoon, John Bloor, bought the name in 1983 and a new factory and range of modern motorcycles followed in the early 1990s. Today, Triumph is one of the few European motorcycling success stories.

Triple treat

Until the launch of the Benelli Tornado at the turn of the millennium, the Triumph three-cylinder engine was unique in a motorcycling world dominated by Japanese fours and European and American twins. In this particular guise, it's a rip-roaring success, delivering a unique blend of fat, flexible torque and high-revving peak power, all to the accompaniment of a quite distinctive exhaust.

Centennial version

A special limited edition 'Centennial' version of the Daytona was launched in the early 2000s to mark Triumph's 100th anniversary. It boasted a special 'British Racing Green' paint job and returned to the use of a smart, single-sided swingarm. This had first been used on the original T595, but was dropped on the 2000+ model.

Soft edged

The Daytona may be a worthy road burner but it has an aging design (based on the original T595 of 1996) and can't match the cutting-edge, up-to-the-minute technology of the very latest superbikes from Japan and Italy. You won't see multi-adjustable inverted forks; radially mounted brake calipers; ultra-lightweight, wavy discs; or LED tail lights here.

Specifications

Engine	Liquid-cooled, four-stroke, transverse three cylinder, DOHC, four valves per cylinder
Chassis	Alloy tubular perimeter
Displacement	955cc
Maximum power	149bhp
Maximum torque	74lb/ft
Transmission	Six gears
Standing quarter mile	11 seconds
Terminal speed	125mph
Maximum speed	161mph
Brakes, front	Nissin; 2 x 320mm front discs, four-piston calipers
Brakes, rear	220mm rear disc, two-piston caliper
Suspension, front	45mm forks, adjustments for pre-load, compression and rebound damping
Suspension, rear	Single shock with rising-rate linkage, adjustments for pre-load, compression and rebound damping
Dry weight	198kg/436lbs
Wheelbase	1,426mm/56.1in
Fuel capacity	20ltr/5.2 US gall
Seat height	815mm/32.1in
Tyres, front	120/70 x 17
Tyres, rear	190/50 x 17
Price	£7,649/US$9,999

If the best means simply the biggest, they don't get any bigger than the 5.7-liter, Chevy V8-engined Boss Hoss

It had to happen... the only surprise is that it happened so many years ago. Weird-engined customs or one-off specials are nothing new in motorcycling, whether they're multi-engined drag bikes or weird and wonderful choppers.

But the biggest of them all, the Boss Hoss, is no one-off. In fact it's been in production, satisfying untold hundreds of buyers, for a full 15 years.

Boss Hoss 350

The core of its appeal is 'That Engine'. The lump that powers the Boss Hoss, and which gives it its unique character, is no ordinary motorcycle engine. In fact it's anything but: it's a car engine. And what a car engine.

The Chevrolet 5.7-liter V8 engine makes 355bhp at a ludicrously low 5,250rpm, with a peak torque of 405lb/ft – or about five times that of a CBR1000RR's lunge – at just 3,500rpm. In the real world, that translates into buckets of lazy grunt that can match almost anything for the first 25 yards or so from the lights.

What's more, this being a Boss Hoss, you can have even more if you want it. A full 502bhp version is available and, if that still isn't sufficient, you can add a turbo and nitrous oxide kit, fully fitted by the factory. This will take the power output to around 1,000bhp. All of this would be about as much use as a bacon sandwich at a bar mitzvah if all that power (and also weight) hadn't been harnessed into a package that handles reasonably well; thankfully the Boss Hoss has been.

Of course, it's no sportsbike, but it's far better through corners than anyone might expect. Lining up for a turn may take a little preparation, (and preferably a wide run-off area, too) but this V8-engined brute handles surprisingly well, thanks mostly to its weight being carried nice and low. Naturally, the brakes, which were upgraded for 2006, help with that; the rear brake is surprisingly powerful. As a result, you have to get used to reducing speed by tapping the rear to keep the bike tracking smoothly through turns.

The Boss Hoss is no high-tech, cutting-edge scalpel. It runs carburetor, not fuel injection, has belt final drive and basic shocks, and you have to look pretty hard to find any 21st century bike technology. On the upside, it boasts massive inverted front forks and the aforementioned latest-spec Brembo brakes. Added to this, there are loads of accessories available.

None of that comes cheap. With even the most basic Boss Hoss starting at $35,000, this is no machine for shrinking violets. But then, it wouldn't be one of the most awesome superbikes on the planet if it was anything else.

From humble beginnings...

Boss Hoss Cycles, Inc. was established in 1990 when Monte Warne, its founder and president, created his first Chevy V-8 powered motorcycle in his 5,000-sq.ft shop in Dyersburg, Tennessee.

...to modern-day success

Over the past 23 years, Boss Hoss Cycles, Inc. has grown from its humble beginnings in Warne's shop to a 22,000-sq.ft manufacturing facility. The product line has also grown from the conventional two-wheeled motorcycle to include three-wheeled vehicles, commonly referred to as trikes.

Keep it simple

The original Boss Hoss was the first V8-powered motorcycle that had the style, look and feel of a traditional cruiser motorcycle. This was accomplished by Warne's unique approach to the motorcycle's single-speed (one-gear) transmission design. The right-angle drive transmission allows the length of the bike to be kept to a minimum, while having the engine mounting in line with the frame made for a well-balanced design that remains unequalled by any other V-8 powered motorcycles.

Modern improvements

The product has seen significant improvements over the years through the research and development efforts of Boss Hoss Cycles' in-house engineering personnel and specialty contractors. Features like a two-speed transmission with reverse; inverted front suspension; vacuum-formed body panels; investment-cast structural frame components, and many other specially designed parts, have helped improve the rigidity and ride of the Boss Hoss motorcycles.

Specifications

Engine	Liquid-cooled Chevrolet V8
Chassis	Tubular steel cradle
Displacement	5,700cc
Maximum power	355bhp
Maximum torque	405lb/ft
Transmission	Two-speed semi-automatic
Standing quarter mile	n/a
Terminal speed	n/a
Maximum speed	130mph
Brakes, front	2 x 12.6in Brembo discs, four-piston calipers
Brakes, rear	12.6in disc, two-piston caliper
Suspension, front	63mm inverted, adjustable for pre-load
Suspension, rear	Twin shocks, adjustable for pre-load
Dry weight	498kg/1,100lbs
Wheelbase	2,032mm/80in
Fuel capacity	32ltr/8.5 US gall
Seat height	711mm/28in
Tyres, front	130/90 x 16
Tyres, rear	230/60 x 15
Price	£n/a/US$35,000

*You can pretty much make your
Boss Hoss anything you
want it to be*

There's weird and wonderful and then there's Harley-powered, fuel-in-frame, rim-disc Buells... and the XB12R Firebolt is Buell's best yet

There's no motorcycle manufacturer quite like Buell... and no Buell quite like the rather unique XB12R Firebolt.

To create the Firebolt, the talismanic company founder and creative force, Erik Buell, took the gloriously offbeat XB9R (which gets its motive force from a 984cc version of the Harley-Davidson 883 Sportster's 45-degree, air-cooled V-twin) and upped the bhp to an ample 103.

Buell XB12R Firebolt

Not all has been changed though the Firebolt retains the XB9R's underslung exhaust and swingarm (which is also cleverly the sump). Most importantly, it also retains XBR9's fun character and sharp steering. But what has been improved is that the bike now has just enough power to push those chassis innovations to the full.

Firing up the XB12R can be harrowing for the uninitiated. At low revs the engine shakes around so much that a rider's vision can literally blur. This shouldn't put you off though because once you head off, the shaking soon disappears.

Not that you will have time to notice because once you twist the throttle and key into the great wads of torque in the lower reaches and a predictable, linear powerband, the XB12R sets off like a scalded cat.

In a nutshell, the XB12R's motor is a truly wonderful street engine. When it comes to power, the XB12R pumps out 92hp at 6,700rpm, a significant 20hp more than the XB9R.

But if the engine – clunky gearbox aside – is a peach, its chassis behavior and handling are better yet. Its ultra-steep 21-degree rake and miniscule 83mm of trail makes for the kind of quick steering never normally found on a 1,200cc machine.

That single front-rim disc is also more powerful than any single disc on a 1,200cc+ machine should be. But then that's the essence of Buell, and the XB12R is its current pinnacle machine. Very little about it is conventional, whether it be the engine, brakes, fuel and oil tanks or the underslung exhaust.

It doesn't all work perfectly, of course. That huge disc brake has a tendency to pull the bike upright if applied through the turns. Also, the bike is more than happy to shoot out exhaust on to your left foot because the side-exit exhaust isn't ideally placed. Finally, the actual fit and finish could be improved throughout – this doesn't have the polish of a Harley-Davidson (who owns the company).

But if you buy a Firebolt, you're getting something fairly unique: clever engineering combined with a measure of exclusivity and performance, and handling that at times simply defies the odds.

In a world where bikes can sometimes feel by-the-numbers, the XB12R Firebolt offers a genuine alternative to such rivals.

That's some brake...

A single 375mm rotor with six-piston caliper is used because it reduces unsprung weight when compared with a twin-disc setup. In addition, the perimeter mounting system isolates the front wheel from most of the braking forces, allowing for a front wheel with thinner spokes, which further reduces the unsprung weight. In practice, it proves to be easy to modulate and has plenty of power for the street. The 240mm rear disc-brake and single-piston caliper isn't very strong, making it easy to modulate without locking the tyre unexpectedly.

And now they're catching on

The XB series appears to be a major hit for Buell. Sales are up 26% in total over 2005, and a company spokesman says the number of units sold through the months of August and September have doubled compared with the same time last year. The American-made sportbikes also appear to be in high demand outside of that continent; more Buells are sold overseas than in the US itself.

Tuning tricks

Torque comes from the Buell's big cylinders, but the linearity of the powerband is due to a couple of tuning tricks. The beautifully shaped, complex bends of the head pipes are up 0.25 inches in diameter from the XB9R to 1.75 inches, allowing for improved flow from the 219cc larger mill. The under-engine exhaust is also different to that of the XB9R as it employs a computer-controlled valve called the Buell Interactive Exhaust. The valve opens at low rpm for the best flow, closes in the mid-range for optimum torque, before opening again at high rpm, responding via throttle position and engine speed.

Harley's little brother

Although Buell started out as an independent company, its links with Harley-Davidson have grown and grown. This led to Harley-Davidson purchasing 97% of the company less than a decade ago. Founder Erik Buell, however, remains an active inspirational force.

Specifications

Engine	Air/oil-cooled, four-stroke, 45-degree V-twin
Chassis	Twin-beam aluminum with fuel in frame
Displacement	1,203cc
Maximum power	100bhp
Maximum torque	81lb/ft
Transmission	Five-speed, belt final drive
Standing quarter mile	12.1 seconds
Terminal speed	117mph
Maximum speed	142mph
Brakes, front	ZTL 375mm rim-mounted disc, six-piston caliper
Brakes, rear	240mm disc, single-piston caliper
Suspension, front	43mm Showa inverted forks with adjustable compression damping, rebound damping and spring pre-load
Suspension, rear	Showa monoshock, pre-load adjust
Dry weight	179kg/395lbs
Wheelbase	1,318mm/51.8in
Fuel capacity	14.5ltr/3.8 US gall
Seat height	775mm/30.5in
Tyres, front	120/70 ZR-17
Tyres, rear	180/55 ZR-17
Price	£7,745/US$10,495

*In a world where bikes can sometimes feel by-the-numbers,
the XB12R Firebolt offers a genuine alternative to such rivals*

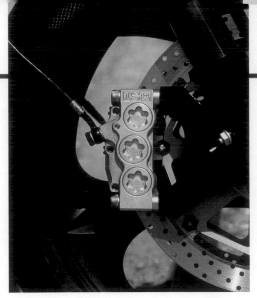

Black magic. Or where the best in US customs blends with the latest technology and a slice of retro chic...

Let's be clear on this – the Confederate Hellcat is a jawdropper from any angle. If you see one in the flesh, you will need to sit down just to let its outlandish looks soak in fully.

Matt Chambers founded Confederate Motorcycles in 1991 to build the ultimate American motorcycle. In 1994, the first Confederates hit the showrooms and to date, a respectable 500 of this original series have been bought by biker fans and they'll be

Confederate F131 Hellcat

delighted to know that another version of the Hellcat is on its way. The hand-made chassis is patented and primed for performance. The Hellcat features a 124 cubic-inch S&S V-Twin engine generating 140hp and a 145lb/ft of torque. You'd better hang on for dear life when you twist that throttle or risk being humiliated in public – albeit in spectacular fashion. Why?

Because all that muscle is crammed into a bike that's practically featherweight.

The Confederate's individuality is reflected by its carbon-fiber solo saddle – it may not be the most comfortable of saddles to endure on a long journey but what the hell, when something looks this good, you can put up with a bit of a numb bum, right? Anyway, look under that seat and you'll discover fully adjustable dual Penske shocks. And the tyres aren't to be sniffed at – they're a set of fat Lightcon wheels with the rear wearing a monsterous 240-section tyre.

The chassis geometry and structural integrity delivers perfectly neutral steering and incredible cruising comfort. The Hellcat has superb handling characteristics and is very smooth. There's very little of the vibration normally associated with a 45-degree V-twin. In fact the whole riding experience is unlike any other V-twin.

But as is the way with the Confederate, its the looks you keep being drawn back to – with its post-modern industrial styling, the bike looks like it could have won World War II single-handed such is its menacing presence. Believe us when we say no one will mistake the Hellcat for a dainty Japanese superbike. Well, that's what the Hellcat makes other bikes look like after all.

When you are riding this bike, you know you are on something different; something truly special, which doesn't feel like it's the five hundred thousandth 'unit' to have rolled off of a faceless production line. But it's not all looks – there is so much torque you could pull out tree stumps. It will carve corners like a sportsbike and will handle anything you can throw at it. Respect it.

Handcrafted or what?

The main frame is also the oil reservoir and the main frame bend gusset is the electrical conduit tunnel. The female seat post is gusseted by the 2-inch conduit tunnel. The swingarm is the exhaust. The entire chassis design is patented and takes 45 hours to build.

Bespoke engines

The engines are manufactured especially for Confederate by S&S. Each motor is built by hand, balanced and blueprinted at S&S before being despatched to the Confederate plant in Louisiana, USA. It's powerful, too. It's claimed that 90bhp reaches the back wheel.

Push my buttons

The switchgear has its head firmly in the future, what with its ergonimically pleasing touchpad that allows you to operate the starting and turn-signal.

Rust? What rust?

The other thing you can't help but notice is all the stainless hardware. What other manufacturer that makes a standard-production vehicle uses only stainless fasteners? All exposed hardware is stainless and could have been polished, yet it remains dull. The exhaust, meanwhile, is ceramic-coated stainless steel.

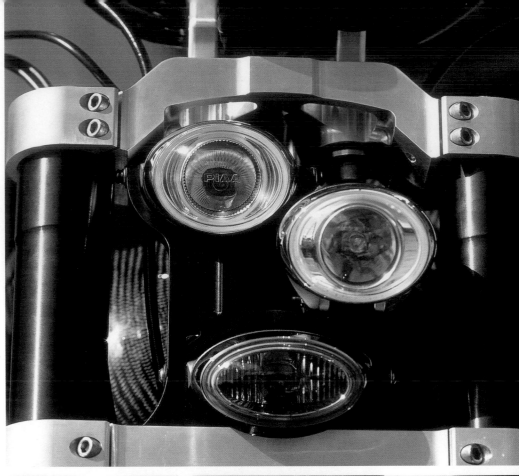

Specifications

Engine	Air-cooled, 45-degree V-twin
Chassis	Tubular steel spine
Displacement	1,600cc
Maximum power	110bhp (est)
Maximum torque	n/a
Transmission	Five gears
Standing quarter mile	n/a
Terminal speed	n/a
Maximum speed	135mph
Brakes, front	2 x 300mm discs, six-piston calipers
Brakes, rear	280mm disc, two-piston caliper
Suspension, front	Marzocchi 50mm inverted front forks
Suspension, rear	Twin Penske shocks, fully-adjustable
Dry weight	222kg/490lbs
Wheelbase	1,575mm/62in
Fuel capacity	n/a
Seat height	n/a
Tyres, front	130/60 x 18
Tyres, rear	240/40 x 18
Price	£n/a/US$67,500

When you are riding this bike, you know you are on something different; something truly special, which doesn't feel like it's the five hundred thousandth 'unit' to have rolled off of a faceless production line

Think you know Harleys? Think again. The V-Rod is the most revolutionary product from the Milwaukee firm in over 50 years...

Harley-Davidson VRSCA V-Rod

Harley-Davidson may be one of the greatest – if not *the* greatest – names in motorcycling, but for a long, long time it wasn't one that made you think of exhilaration and hardcore performance. That all changed with the mighty V-Rod in 2001.

Put bluntly, this cycle is quick – seriously quick – spinning its rear tyre away from the lights with an engine that keeps pulling way beyond where a traditional, air-cooled Milwaukee V-Harley has run out of breath. To deliver all that, it'll come as no surprise that the V-Rod is different to any other Harley you've seen. And that's because, at the heart of the V-Rod, is an engine like no other that has ever come on a Harley.

The liquid-cooled V-twin (a Harley first) was jointly developed with Porsche Engineering and is derived from the VR1000 superbike that raced in the USA's AMA Superbike Championship. And, although it's no nimble superbike like those pouring out of Japan, its 1,130cc engine can still put out a credible 115bhp.

That motor is something special and without such a pedigree, the V-Rod would never have blessed our roads with its presence. It takes a cattle prod to any notions you may have about the Harley experience and gives them a darn good poking.

The first way of riding this monster bike, is to leave the revs down low and ride the V-Rod's 74lb/ft torque by short-shifting through the slick five-speed gearbox out of every corner. However, if short-shifting isn't your thing, you can also ride the V-Rod just like any other modern superbike and rev it right to the redline. The motor has a very real kick at the top end and is also utterly smooth and quiet, all of which is the complete antithesis to the delivery of conventional Harley-Davidsons.

That motor, however, isn't the only chapter in the V-Rod story. Everything about it is different to Harleys of yore. For a start it's full of aluminum (rather than cast iron and steel), it's got a radiator (due to the liquid-cooling, again a Harley first), the styling is fresh, and it handles well, too.

At first, the V-Rod takes a great deal of getting used to. With its laid-back riding position where the back of the seat rests against your lower back and your feet are forward, chopper-style, your position doesn't make the V-Rod feel like it's ready to rip up chunks out of the highway.

Despite the relaxed steering and fork angle where the forks look like they're a few feet in front of you when you're riding, the V-Rod turns beautifully. Yes, you have to watch yourself on the corners because of the lack of ground clearance, but still, you can move from left to right with astonishing ease – quite a feat for a bike with such a long wheelbase.

The V-Rod is a real credit to Harley Davidson who claim that they were pondering making this bike as far back as 1995. The fact we all had to wait so long to see the fruits of their labor finally hit the showrooms is the only downside to this bold and very modern move. Whoever said that Harley were stuck in their ways should start eating some serious humble pie. Make ours two slices...

Breaking the mould

Harley call the engine the 'Revolution', and, especially in the context of Harley engines that have gone before, that's not overstating the mark. With liquid-cooling, double overhead cams and four valves per cylinder, it's chalk and cheese compared with Harley's air-cooled, pushrod, traditional fare.

My other bike's a Porsche

If the Harley brand isn't a big enough pull, the V-Rod has one other name of distinction hiding under a bushel. The Revolution engine wasn't actually built in-house in Milwaukee; it was engineered and developed by Porsche in Germany who, apparently, know a thing or two about performance engines.

Dig those curves

This is no average exhaust. The two-into-two, gorgeously styled, side-swept pipes are an irregular curved shape compared with conventional 'straight-through' exhausts, formed via a novel (and very expensive) hydro-forming process.

Look ma, no paint

The original V-Rod from 2001 came in one color only – silver. But this wasn't any old silver... it was no-paint-polished alloy silver. If any machine looked like it was carved out of solid aluminum billet, this was it.

Specifications

Engine	Fuel-injected, DOHC, eight-valve 60-degree V-twin
Chassis	Steel tube double cradle
Displacement	1,130cc
Maximum power	115bhp
Maximum torque	65lb/ft
Transmission	Five-speed, belt final drive
Standing quarter mile	11.2 seconds
Terminal speed	122mph
Maximum speed	139mph
Brakes, front	2 x 292mm discs, four-piston calipers
Brakes, rear	292 disc, four-piston caliper
Suspension, front	49mm telescopic forks
Suspension, rear	Twin shocks, pre-load adjustable
Dry weight	270kg/594lbs
Wheelbase	1,750mm/68.9in
Fuel capacity	18ltr/4.75 US gall
Seat height	660mm/26in
Tyres, front	120/70 x 19
Tyres, rear	180/50 x 18
Price	£12,850/US$15,995

*The V-Rod is like no Harley
you've ever seen before...*

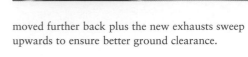

The world had barely got used to the V-Rod when Harley decided to push the boundaries even further

Look over the Street Rod and it doesn't take an overqualified, chin-stroking product designer to figure out that its DNA is heavily shared with the respected V-Rod. But there is a key difference that underlines Harley's ambitions when they created the Street Rod variant.

It's been constructed to suit the more European tastes among the biking fraternity – in other words, it's got some serious cornering ability.

Harley-Davidson VRSCR Street Rod

Nestled in a hydro-formed, tubular perimeter frame sits the 1,130cc, 60-degree Revolution V-twin engine. It's largely unchanged, but Harley claims a better exhaust and remapped fuel injection boosts power to 120hp at 8,500rpm, 5hp better than it claimed for the original V-Rod Twin.

Although the engine is little different, however, that certainly can't be said about the bike's rolling chassis. Brembo were commissioned to create four-piston brakes and Harley has sharpened up the steering. To aid with cornering and give the rider a more sporting feel when astride the Street Rod, the seat is now higher with the footpegs

moved further back plus the new exhausts sweep upwards to ensure better ground clearance.

Alas, for all these improvements, Street Rod owners shouldn't start kidding themselves that their American icon will start putting the wind up the Japanese hardcore sportsbikes just yet – or it could be time for some serious egg on the face. This is still a bike that's low-slung, lardy and rather long compared to its svelte competitors.

The Street Rod just hasn't the cubes to compete with the latest generation of power cruisers, such as Triumph's Rocket III. A twist of the wrist doesn't immediately jerk the bike forward – in fact, the hit off the bottom is rather mild. But once the needle on the tach rises to 5,000rpm, the power comes on strong and gets the 650lb steed moving in a hurry.

But the thrill of the Street Rod isn't so much in any new internal workings but, rather, in the redesign of the overall chassis. Its more upright riding position allows for aggressive riding thanks to new suspension all round and a change in the fork angle. This is now a reasonable 32 degrees instead of the chopper-like 38 degrees of the V-Rod. The forks, meanwhile, have been upgraded to 43mm inverted items in place of the V-Rod's 49mm conventional forks – and they absorb bumps and dips sweetly while providing impressive stability in the twists. Finally, the wheelbase was reduced by 0.7inches to allow for greater maneuverability. Overall, the Street Rod is still no GSX-R-chaser, but it's far removed from any traditional Harley. It takes a little muscle to lean it into a corner, but when it gets there the Street Rod stays planted.

Harley-Davidson took a chance with the V-Rod. With the Street Rod, it pushed the barriers even further with a more performance-based design. The Street Rod is a triumphant blend of Harley-Davidson styling and adrenaline-injected, blood-pumping performance.

Improved brakes

What brings the Street Rod to a stop is a set of improved brakes. While Hayes discs graced the original V-Rod, for the Street Rod, Harley-Davidson upgraded to a set of Brembo four-piston calipers in the front and a single 300mm rotor out back. The upgrades pay huge dividends on the road and provide ample stopping power.

Are we sitting comfortably?

Ergonomically, the Street Rod is very comfortable. Arms are splayed out in front at a very reasonable position, which allows the rider to either hunch forward when playing sportbike rider or sit back and enjoy the scenery. Feet rest comfortably on the pegs, directly below the hips and a bit behind the knees.

Saddle sore

The saddle feels rather firm at first touch, but is remarkably comfortable when riding for long periods of time. The seat position is much more 'on top' of the bike than its cruiser cousin, which allows a rider to climb around the saddle to adjust weight and balance for those sharp blacktop benders. Look underneath the lockless seat and you'll find the 5.0-gallon fuel cell, up significantly from the pitifully puny 3.7-gallon tank in the V-Rod.

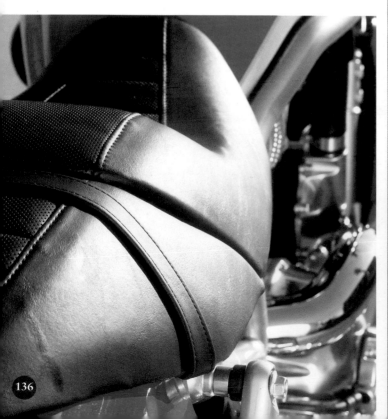

Specifications

Engine	Fuel-injected, DOHC, eight-valve, 60-degree V twin
Chassis	Tubular steel double cradle
Displacement	1,130cc
Maximum power	120bhp
Maximum torque	80lb/ft
Transmission	Five-speed, belt final drive
Standing quarter mile	11.1 seconds
Terminal speed	124mph
Maximum speed	147mph
Brakes, front	2 x 300mm discs, four-piston calipers
Brakes, rear	300mm disc, four-piston caliper
Suspension, front	Inverted 43mm forks
Suspension, rear	Twin shocks, pre-load adust
Dry weight	293kg/645lbs
Wheelbase	1,700mm/66.9in
Fuel capacity	18.9ltr/5 US gall
Seat height	762mm/31in
Tyres, front	120/70 x 19
Tyres, rear	180/55 x 18
Price	£10,995/US$15,495

The Titan Motorcycle Company claims it was born from the cult of the big, all-American V-Twin motorcycles immortalized in movies like 'The Wild Ones', 'Easy Rider' and 'Electra Glide in Blue'. And who are we to argue with them?

When is a custom-built, hand-crafted superbike a manufactured product you can buy from a dealer? When it's a Titan

Founded in 1994, Titan set out to design custom, volume-produced, performance, American-made, V-twin-engined motorcycles, and they've succeeded in grand fashion.

Titan Gecko

Since Titan's launch 22 years ago in Phoenix, Arizona, USA, many other custom bike 'manufacturers' have sprung up, particularly in the States, to varying degrees of success. But Titan is the firm that started it all.

Making between 500 and 600 bikes a year, Titan wants to appeal to a different consumer than Harley-Davidson, who produce hundreds of

thousands of bikes annually. This is also shown in the price tag; the Titan line-up currently ranges from $32,000 to the top of the line, custom rubber-mount chopper selling for $45,000. In other words, Titan produces bespoke custom bikes tailored to your preferences from a massive options list, bristling with the very best in motorcycle and custom componentry.

The catalogue is impressive. From soft tails with air-ride suspensions to rigid frames with springer front ends, the American company offers it all. The base models are the Gecko, Roadrunner, Sidewinder and Phoenix. Most customers, however, will treat those bikes as a base, a blank canvas, which they then customize to suit their own tastes.

Naturally enough, no two Titans, let alone Geckos, are identical. Essentially, however, the Gecko is the long, low-rider of the range; it's characterized by a low seat, skinny front tyre and kicked-out front forks. But that's just the start. At the heart of it, usually, is a 112-cubic-inch S&S V-twin engine capable of pumping out 120hp. That gets transmitted to the ground (again, nothing is ever certain with Titans) through a massive 250mm rear tyre. Add to that Titan's own four-inch stretched, rubber-mounted frame and three-piece swingarm (complete with hidden axle covers) plus Performance Machine brakes, mag wheels, a stretched one-piece tank/seat unit, chrome Titan handlebars and controls, a Headwinds headlight, skirted front finder, and you've got the basic ingredients of the Gecko.

If all of that sounds like a feast fit for a king, you're not far wrong. After all, the Gecko is not just a performance machine *par excellence*, it's also a motorcycling jewel and is revered as such throughout the motorcycling world. Prepare to bow in front of its greatness.

It's all in the detail

One indication of Titan's thoroughness is that each bike's frame is color-matched when powder-coated to the bike's paint scheme, whatever that may be.

Decisions, decisions...

The best of the custom world's component parts fill Titan's catalogue: Performance Machine (PM) brakes and wheels, S&S motors and much more. Does is turn us into overgrown kids in a candy store? Of course it does...

How fast?

The Gecko may not look like a performance machine, but with 120bhp on tap from the big bore 112-cubic-inch S&S motor, it's certainly no slouch. If you can hang on, reckon on a top speed heading for 130mph (depending on gearing) and a standing quarter mile time in the low 11s.

Specifications

Engine	S&S air-cooled 45-degree V-twin
Chassis	Steel tube double cradle
Displacement	112 cubic inch
Maximum power	120bhp
Maximum torque	n/a
Transmission	Five gears
Standing quarter mile	n/a
Terminal speed	n/a
Maximum speed	n/a
Brakes, front	13in disc, six-piston Performance Machine caliper
Brakes, rear	11.5in disc, four-piston caliper
Suspension, front	54mm Titan inverted forks
Suspension, rear	Twin shocks
Dry weight	288kg/635lbs
Wheelbase	1,778mm/70in
Fuel capacity	17ltr/4.5 US gall
Seat height	628mm/24.75in
Tyres, front	90/90 x 21
Tyres, rear	200/55 x 18
Price	£n/a/US$32,000

There's more to American superbikes than Harley-Davidson. Victory is the new kid on the block and growing fast...

Victory Hammer

Harley-Davidson is probably the biggest brand in motorcycling but there's another US company which is causing waves and is in danger of becoming an icon too if it continues to trailblaze its way across the biking world as it has been – it's Victory Motorcycles and the Hammer.

Size matters at Victory Motorcycles and they've underlined this fact by fitting the Hammer with the largest rear tyre ever put on a mass-produced bike – coming in at a whopping 250mm, the back tyre is a colossus.

But as we all know, quantity is nothing without quality and the Hammer isn't left lacking in this department either. You only need to check out the Hammer's snorting engine to know that the bike means business.

It's fitted with the company's new Freedom 100/6 V-twin engine and Victory claims the 1,634cc motor has 22% more torque and is 10% more powerful than the engine featured in the Hammer's forebears, the Kingpin and the Vegas.

In practice, the Hammer's motor has plenty of torque on offer and can start dishing out the power with utter ease from low down in the rev range. And, although it's vibey like any big V-twin, there is now a sixth gear that makes cruising an absolute cinch.

As is the way with US bikes though, you always end up coming back to what's on display. With that huge tyre on the rear, the spectacle is almost too much as a Hammer roars past you on the highway – that back tyre simply looks too big but a split second later and the penny drops as the Hammer's epic rear proportions suddenly make sense. This is a bike that wants and more importantly deserves to be noticed.

Of course, with such a huge tyre in place, there's bound to be repercussions on the bike's handling and the Hammer cannot be described as having pitch-perfect cornering manners.

Never mind though because what the Hammer does offer is an utterly predictable and welcoming riding experience, which is aided by that new sixth gear.

And speed freaks will find that the Hammer's acceleration is more than enough to plant a fixed grin (very) wide across the face – the Hammer is no wannabe.

All in all, the Victory Hammer offers up a unique experience for the buyer. That tyre, that 100+bhp plus the all-American styling means its maker could yet still find itself moving up the food chain.

Most importantly, Victory Motorcycles could well find itself in the position one day to give King Harley a right royal (and rather rude) shove off its throne. Only time will tell if Victory can deliver that Hammer blow...

Bigger... times two

The Hammer is the first Victory to displace 100 cubic inches (that's 1,634cc for the metrically inclined) and sport a six-speed transmission with a true overdrive. To give riders the freedom to use that more powerful engine, the crankcase is actually 10mm narrower than the current 1,500cc engine. This one change gives two degrees more ground clearance on both sides of the bike.

Uprated suspension

A cartridge fork and single rear shock handle the suspension duties. Slowing comes courtesy of a pair of 300mm front discs and Brembo four-piston calipers. Stretched between the 18 x 3.0-inch front wheel and the 18 x 8.5-inch rear, the Hammer carries an inverted fork and a swoopy styling – including a sportbike-type passenger-seat cowl – that makes the motorcycle look fast even when the engine is switched off.

Cancelled out

We all want them so we all want to know why more manufacturers aren't providing them – self-cancelling signals that is. The Hammer is blessed with them so why aren't more bike makers offering them?

Specifications

Engine	Fuel-injected, four-stroke, 50 degree V-twin SOHC, four valves per cylinder
Chassis	Steel tube double cradle
Displacement	1,634cc
Maximum power	n/a
Maximum torque	n/a
Transmission	Six-speed, belt final drive
Standing quarter mile	11.9 secomds
Terminal speed	119mph
Maximum speed	134mph
Brakes, front	300mm disc, four-piston caliper
Brakes, rear	300mm disc, four-piston caliper
Suspension, front	43mm inverted forks
Suspension, rear	Monoshock with pre-load adjust
Dry weight	298kg/657lbs
Wheelbase	1,668mm/65.7in
Fuel capacity	17ltr/4.5 US gall
Seat height	669mm/26.4in
Tyres, front	130/70 x 18
Tyres, rear	250/40 x 18
Price	£n/a/US$16,899

*With that huge tyre on the rear, the
spectacle is almost too much as a
Hammer roars past you on the
highway – that back tyre simply
looks too big but a split second
later and the penny drops as the
Hammer's truly epic rear
proportions suddenly
make sense*

The Future
of the Superbike

Every year motorcyclists the world over wonder how the
following year's superbikes could possibly get any better.
Today's machines are already almost as fast as F1 cars, yet
often as easy to ride as novice machines. One thing that's
certain is that superbikes will become faster still, more
refined, easier to ride and possibly wackier, too. A recent
trend throughout motorcycling has been for wilder styling
and bolder concepts. So, expect more variety, more attitude
and more radical use of the latest technologies.

Space-age styling, high-tech gizmos and, yes, six cylinders. Best of all, though, it may yet become a reality...

Remember the Katana? Suzuki's wild-styled (by Jan Felstrom of German design house Target) silver superbike of the early to mid-1980s? Well in these times of 'everything retro', it looks like the Katana is back – at least if Suzuki's latest concept machine, the Stratosphere, is anything to go by.

The Stratosphere was unveiled at the 2005 Tokyo Motorcycle Show, which is traditionally a prestige event for manufacturers to showcase their

Suzuki Stratosphere

forthcoming technologies. Not only is the Stratosphere a remarkably complete and rounded machine, but Suzuki has something of a reputation for turning its concept bikes into reality. For the evidence look no further than its B-King concept machine. This first morphed into the GSR600 roadster, launched in 2006, and is set to be followed up by a full-bore 1,300cc version in 2007. And when – not if – the Stratosphere does appear in the metal, it looks like we're in for something of a treat.

First there's that styling – influenced in part by the Katanas of 20 years ago, but also, according to Suzuki, said to represent a jet at high speed above the earth, hence the name. The Stratosphere's profile from fuel tank to rear seat, meanwhile, 'expresses an image like the backside of a human being'. Quite. Elsewhere, the radiator side-covers use 'Damascus steel with unique surface pattern to introduce a touch of mystical feel to motorcycle design'. Starting to get the idea?

All that flouncy bodywork is wrapped around the first six-cylinder motorcycle engine from a major manufacturer since the Z1300 and CBX behemoths from Kawasaki and Honda at the end of the 1970s. The major difference here, however, is that the Stratosphere's power unit is anything but massive. Due to what Suzuki calls a "space-saving design", the Stratosphere's 1,100cc six is claimed to be as compact as a typical four of the same displacement, and slightly narrower than its own GSX1400.

There's more, too. There are neat touches throughout the riding compartment, the centerpiece being a trick-looking multi-function display tucked behind an electrically adjustable windscreen. The handlebars and pillion footrests are also height adjustable to suit all sizes. There is an electronic wheel-lock security device, keyless engine start (now commonplace in the automotive world), while four LED headlamps are positioned up front. And if all that's not enough, there are even blue indirect lighting strips positioned down the frame side and under the center of the fuel tank for a touch of the phantasmal special effects.

It's unlikely, of course, that all of that will reach any final production version. At least, not for a while. But some of it will, and soon. There is a strong likelihood that the Stratosphere's six-cylinder engine will form the basis of the next generation Suzuki Hayabusa. Increasingly adjustable riding positions are already with us, mostly thanks to BMW. And as for the styling, who knows? But it's going to be a helluva lot of fun finding out...

Automatic for the people

The Stratosphere's transmission can be run in either automatic or manual mode, with manual taking over whenever the clutch is engaged. This autoshift mechanism, which retains the clutch lever (unlike Yamaha's recent FJR1300S tourer), was a result of Suzuki's conclusion that, in order to preserve the joy of motorcycle operation, they "needed to retain human input, rather than using automation to simply pursue ease of use".

Flight deck

The café racer-style handlebars may look low tech, but the instrument display is anything but. Instead of an analog dial, the Suzuki Stratosphere uses an LCD that can show a variety of information. Control buttons are conveniently located around the tank's filler cap, and the Plexiglas windscreen even has up and down positions for different riding styles.

You've been framed

Is this the gizmo to end all gizmos? At the front of the Stratosphere, attached next to the headlight, is a video camera... a little extra something so you can record your rides "adding to enjoyment after getting off the bike".

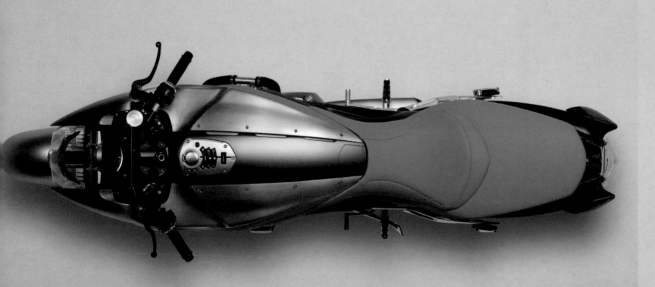

Specifications

Engine	Liquid-cooled, four-stroke DOHC transverse six
Chassis	Tubular steel
Displacement	1,100cc
Maximum power	180bhp
Maximum torque	n/a
Transmission	Semi-automatic
Standing quarter mile	n/a
Terminal speed	n/a
Maximum speed	n/a
Brakes, front	2 discs, six-piston calipers
Brakes, rear	Single disc, two-piston caliper
Suspension, front	Telescopic forks, fully adjustable
Suspension, rear	Single shock, fully adjustable
Dry weight	n/a
Wheelbase	n/a
Fuel capacity	n/a
Seat height	n/a
Tyres, front	n/a
Tyres, rear	n/a
Price	n/a

The ultimate racer replica is on its way...

Ducati's long-rumored, road-going replica of its awesome Desmosedici MotoGP machine is set for limited, ultra-exclusive production beginning in 2007. Simply put, Ducati claims this will be the highest-performance production motorcycle available. Production will be limited to 400 bikes per year.

The Desmosedici RR derives most of its technology from the GP6, currently being raced in the 2006 MotoGP World Championship. Like

Ducati Desmosedici RR

the racer, the RR's engine has Ducati's traditional desmodromic valve control matched to a 989cc four-cylinder 'L' layout. The double overhead cams are gear driven, while the six-speed transmission retains its 'racing' characteristics by being cassette type, and featuring a hydraulically actuated dry multi-plate slipper clutch.

Construction is also to MotoGP standard. There are sand-cast, aluminum crankcase and cylinder

heads, titanium connecting rods and valves, and sand-cast magnesium engine covers. It's all enough, Ducati claim, for a mind-boggling 200bhp with the optional 102-decibel racing silencer and dedicated CPU race kit fitted.

The technological wizardry also extends to the chassis. Ducati's signature tubular trellis hybrid frame is used. Attached to that is a carbon-fiber rear seat support while the RR also sports a new, extra-long cast, forged and pressed aluminum alloy swingarm. The geometry and the technology of this are taken directly from the MotoGP machine and give the RR excellent weight distribution as well as a superb stiffness-to-weight ratio.

Suspension-wise, the RR features some of the most advanced components available. The rear suspension layout is the same as that of the GP6, with the rear shock attached above the swingarm and to a rocker, which is hinged to the crankcase.

The suspension comprises 43mm upside-down Ohlins FG353 forks, which are normally only used in competition, that are adjustable for pre-load, rebound and compression. The rear shock is also Ohlins and has rebound, low/high-speed compression adjustment and hydraulic pre-load adjustment.

The list of racing components used, however, doesn't stop there. The RR features Brembo radial 'monoblock' brake calipers, a radial master cylinder with hinged lever and remote 'quick' adjuster. In addition, the two front brake discs are the same as those used on the GP6 racer in its wet weather race set-up, namely two semi-floating 320mm discs with a 240mm fixed disc and a two-piston floating caliper.

And if all that doesn't make the mind boggle, a special race kit will also be available. As well as the aforementioned 102-decibel racing exhaust and dedicated CPU, this will include a bike cover and paddock stand. Start queuing now...

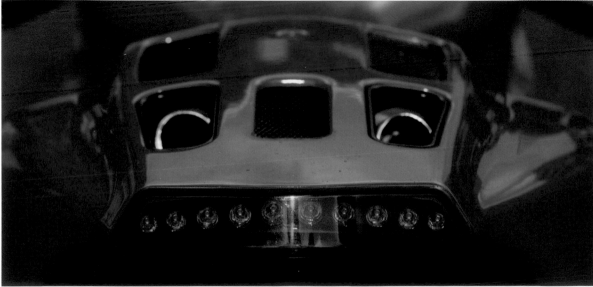

Specifications

Engine	Liquid-cooled, DOHC, desmodromic V4, fuel-injected
Chassis	Tubular steel trellis hybrid, carbon-fiber seat, support, aluminum swingarm
Displacement	989cc
Maximum power	200bhp
Maximum torque	n/a
Transmission	Six gears
Standing quarter mile	n/a
Terminal speed	n/a
Maximum speed	200mph
Brakes, front	2 x semi-floating 320mm x 6r discs, Brembo radial monoblo calipers
Brakes, rear	240mm disc, two-piston floati caliper
Suspension, front	Ohlins "FG353" PFF forks U 43mm pressurized, with pre-lo rebound and compression adjustment, TiN-coated sliders
Suspension, rear	Ohlins rear shock, with rebou low/high speed compression adjustment, and hydraulic pre-load adjustment
Dry weight	n/a
Wheelbase	n/a
Fuel capacity	n/a
Seat height	n/a
Tyres, front	n/a
Tyres, rear	n/a
Price	£37,500/US$65,000